How They Linger

"This book is a sure cure for cynicism and a remedy for depression. Some of the stories are vintage favorites. Others are classics-in-the-making. Each spotlights a life well lived that remains bright in Davis' memory."

—**Elizabeth Ellis,** Circle of Excellence storyteller and author of *Every Day a Holiday*

"*How They Linger* is a lovely example of "memento morti" as only Donald Davis can write it with his familiar mix of humor, wistfulness, and a deep appreciation for Appalachian culture. The chapters are simultaneously a collection of stories he has told from the stage and a set of recollections of people who made a difference in his life that Donald does not want to forget, or have us forget once we have read these chapters. *How They Linger* is pure Donald Davis on the page."

—**Loren Niemi,** former Chair of the National Storytelling Network and co-founder of the American School of Storytelling

"*How They Linger* takes readers on a delightful dive into kind and vividly varied times, into a world of beloved, quirky relatives and neighbors, childhood friends reclaimed and rediscovered, even wise and preternaturally forgiving animals. These stories can inspire us all to find our own treasured memories—and to tell them."

—**Jo Radner,** past president of the American Folklore Society and the National Storytelling Network

"A powerful collection of stories of people you may have otherwise mistaken as ordinary."

—**Bil Lepp,** storyteller and author

How They Linger

Stories of unforgettable souls

Donald Davis

Author of *Tales of a Free-Range Childhood*

Parkhurst Brothers Publishers
MARION, MICHIGAN

www.parkhurstbrothers.com

Consumers may order Parkhurst Brothers books from their favorite online or brick-and-mortar booksellers, expecting prompt delivery. Parkhurst Brothers books are distributed to the trade through the Chicago Distribution Center. Trade and library orders may be placed through Ingram Book Company, Baker & Taylor, Follett Library Resources, and other book industry wholesalers. To order from Chicago Distribution Center, phone 1-800-621-2736 or fax to 800-621-8476. Copies of this and other Parkhurst Brothers Publishers titles are available to organizations and corporations for purchase in quantity by contacting the Special Sales Department at our home office location, listed on our website. Manuscript submission guidelines for this publishing company are available at our website.

Printed in the United States of America
First Edition, March 2024
Printing history: 2026 2025 2024 12 11 10 9 8 7 6 5 4 3 2 1

Library Cataloging Data:
1. Davis, Donald, 1944–Childhood and youth.
2. North Carolina–Social life and customs.
3. Authors, American–20th century Biography.
4 Davis, Donald, 1944–Family.
5. Title
813:54

ISBN: Trade Paperback   978-1-62491-200-9
ISBN: e-book   978-1-62491-201-6

Parkhurst Brothers Publishers believes that the free and open exchange of ideas is essential for the maintenance of our freedoms. We support the First Amendment of the United States Constitution and encourage all citizens to study all sides of public policy questions, making up their own minds.

Cover and interior design by   Linda D. Parkhurst, PhD
Acquired for Parkhurst Brothers Publishers and edited by: Ted Parkhurst
Cover art: Adobe Stock 299583549

022024

For Trish,

Who keeps helping me to become myself.

Contents

A Prologue

BACK AT THE BEGINNING OF COVID, when we were in extended residence at home, I was reading one day about concepts of death in different cultures around the world. One of those concepts concerned death in certain Sub-Saharan cultures on the African continent.

Where we, in the West, have but two concepts of death, you are either dead or alive; in these cultures, there exists a third concept: we might call it "the living dead."

The living dead is that category composed of all those people whose biology has expired, but who continue to be remembered, talked about, and whose stories continue to be told. In those sub-Saharan cultures, a person is not considered "dead" until their stories cease to be told by living descendants and friends.

This made me think about all of those people who compose my personal list of "living dead." More specifically, it sparked my thinking about those people whom I remember and can tell stories about who, by now, have been forgotten by others. Is it even possible, I thought, that there are some people about whom only I might tell a story? Are there some people who would be totally dead if I did not tell about them?

That thought was the origin of this book. It is made up of stories, some of which I have told, some of which I might tell, some of which I would only seldom tell, that could come from no one else but me. This quest involved a lot of thinking, even more remembering, and eventually making many lists of people otherwise long forgotten.

Eventually, I began to put the stories together in writing. Some of the stories I had actually told in the past, but I had never written. A wide range of personalities are being kept alive in these stories. They range from musicians to a town drunk to a murder victim. The things my subjects have in common are that they are all people who deserve to be remembered and, perhaps, that only I still hold on to these particular stories about them.

The eventual title came one day when the members of a men's quartet with whom I sing on the island (The Holy Mackerels) were making up a list of songs we might sing at the annual OcraFolk Music and Storytelling Festival. One of the songs under consideration in my mind was J. B. F. Wright's "Precious Memories." As soon as the words started to run through my mind, "Precious memories, how they linger ..." I realized that they were describing this story project. So, *How They Linger,* became the book's title. The people who inhabit these stories never leave me. I hope my telling about them honors and keeps them among the living dead just a little bit longer.

Chapter One
Aunt Mary

I AM NOT SURE WHETHER I ACTUALLY REMEMBER the day my Aunt Mary came to stay with us or whether I have heard the story told so many times I just think I remember it.

She and Uncle Gudger had been recently married. He had been sent overseas in the army following the end of World War II. At this time, they did not yet have a home of their own, and she was living alone in the old house on the family farm, the place that had been empty since my Grandmother Davis had died in 1943.

It was Aunt Mary's first year teaching school, and this living arrangement required her to drive her old black Plymouth sixteen miles from the farm into town each day to get to her school. At that time, more than half of those miles were still unpaved roads.

One night my parents had invited her to come to our house for supper after she was all finished at school. This was a fairly regular invitation.

That night, it started pouring rain about the time she arrived, and the rain continued to pour down harder and harder as supper progressed. (The rain is the part I'm quite sure I remember.)

When we finished eating, my Daddy issued the invitation: "Mary, don't try to drive home in the dark in all of this rain. Just stay and spend the night with us. It won't hurt you to wear the same clothes to school two days in a row ... Some of your children probably wear the same clothes for a week."

So, she spent the night with us ... for about the next two years!

For me, it was like having a second mother, only better! It was my Mama's job to raise me, feed me, clothe me, and discipline me; it was Aunt Mary's job to try to undo the discipline and spoil me totally rotten. It was a beautiful thing! For some reason, at my age, I called her "Aunt Dye-dye," and that name stuck for most of my growing-up years.

My earliest real memories of her are our walks after supper on many nights. We would finish our family meal and, as my mother gathered up the dishes to wash them, instead of offering to help, Aunt Mary would offer, "Why don't I take the baby for a walk while you do the dishes?"

The only problem with this offer for me is that my Aunt Mary had never walked a single step in her entire life. She ran in a little trot everywhere she went. She would take my hand,

and we would head across the front yard and out to unpaved Plott Creek Road. Even running, I could not keep up with her. By the time we had reached the road, she had given up on my walking and hoisted me onto one of her hips to carry me.

We were going on what she called "a two-hip walk." We would walk up Plott Creek Road until her first hip was worn out; then she would shift me to the opposite hip for the down-hill return home.

It is a strange thing how memories work. Logically I know that it cannot be true that—just as we turned around on each of those nights—the first star came out. It just seems that way to me. I suspect that, according to the time of year, she was looking for that first star to mark our turning around place.

We would both be looking to see who could spot the first star. When one of us saw it, we would cry out, "There it is!" Then Aunt Mary would set me down on the ground, often at the edge of an open field beside the road, and we would circle holding hands and looking up while she chanted:

> *Mica, mica, parva stella;*
> *Miror quaenam sis tam bella.*
> *Splendens eminus in illo,*
> *Alba velut gemma caelo.*

I chanted the sounds phonetically with her until—in no time—we were saying them together. It seemed like we were wizards or witches of some kind as we chanted over and over again while more stars popped out. It was not until I was in

11

high school Latin that I learned we had been reciting "Twinkle, Twinkle, Little Star" in Latin!

When we had chanted sufficiently, she would pick me up and say: "Time to make a wish…Star light, star bright, first star I see tonight, I wish I may I wish I might have this wish I wish tonight." We would then each pick our own personal first star, close our eyes, and make our wishes.

I often asked Aunt Mary what she wished for, and she answered: "You can't tell your wish, or it will not come true." This explained why almost none of the things I wished for ever happened: I could not keep from telling about them, which surely jinxed it. But as I watched her lips move silently while her eyes were closed, I could always see tears running down her cheeks as she wished. Much later, I realized that she had been wishing that Uncle Gudger would come home safe from his overseas tour of duty.

As we walked back toward the house, now with me on the opposite hip, she would often tell me: "Remember, there is a star in the sky for every baby who has ever been born in this world. And there is already a star there for every baby who will ever be born. Do you know what our job is?"

I knew the answer; "It is to figure out which star is ours because our star holds our destiny" (a word I repeated from her without knowing what it meant). I would look and look at the stars, trying to decide which one I thought was mine. A large star would be my choice, but later, I would realize that all the prominent stars had probably already been taken by people who lived before us. With that in mind, I picked a tiny star, hoping it was so small that no one else might have noticed it. The problem with that was, once I had chosen a small star, I could never find it again!

I would ask Aunt Mary, "Which star is yours?"

She would answer. "Oh, you can't tell that ... it has to be a secret."

Then, one night, as we were walking back, a brilliant shooting star crossed the sky. Suddenly I knew the answer: that has to be *her star* because it's the one that can't stand still. It has to run everywhere it goes!

Aunt Mary had a black 1939 Plymouth that she had bought when she was hired for her first job at the end of World War II. When they got married, Uncle Gudger had a black 1939 Ford. Since she already had her own car when he was overseas, she did not need to use his.

Before he shipped out, he took the black Ford out to his brother, G. C.'s house, to leave it there for safekeeping. The two of them washed and waxed the Ford and stored it in the big barn. They raised the car up on blocks and let the air out of the tires so they wouldn't be under pressure.

They removed the spark plugs and poured oil into the cylinder heads. Then they replaced the spark plugs. They knew they would need to drain the old fuel out of the gas tank, refill it, and blow out the fuel lines before starting it back up after Gudger got home. With all of this done, they covered the car with an olive-drab canvas tarp and tied the tarp down for safe-keeping. Once in a while, Mary and my Daddy would stop off at G. C.'s house to check on the car so when she wrote to Uncle Gudger, she could tell him that all was well.

A few months after Gudger left, during a huge storm, lightning hit the barn. It caught fire and burned to the ground. The Ford burned with it.

When Aunt Mary learned of the fire, she was distraught. "I know how he loved that car," she moaned. "I don't know if he loved me that much or not. After all, I was supposed to look out for it." She was nervous about writing her next letter in which she would have to tell him about the fate of his car.

Once the letter went in the mail, she was scared to hear back from him. They had never had an argument or a dis-agreement in their short marriage, and she was afraid that this would be the beginning of his disappointment in her.

Finally, the reply came. Mary was so scared to open the letter and read it that she had my Daddy open it and read it to her. When he did so, he was surprised to discover that instead of using all the available paper to tell her as much about what was happening to him as possible, the letter was made up of a single sentence. Daddy read it aloud to all of us: "Dear Mary, Don't worry about the car...I didn't like the horn anyway. But I love you, Gudger." In later years as I came to know Uncle

Gudger well, I realized that his attitude about the importance of people over things would govern his entire personality.

Aunt Mary loved to sing and dance. She carried me around the house singing songs like "Soloman Levi," "Captain Jinks," "Too Old to Cut the Mustard," "Just Because," "Oh Lonesome Me," "MacNamra's Band"," Oh My Darling Clementine", and many others. We would dance around from room to room as she sang,

> Oh, I'm Captain Jinks of the Horse Marines,
> I feed my horse on corn and beans,
> I often live beyond my means,
> as a Captain in the Army...

I absorbed all of those songs!

Aunt Mary always saved one special song for the full moon. When that night came, Aunt Mary and I would go out in the front yard, look up at the moon, and she would sing and dance around to "Buffalo Gals." The problem was that she never could remember the words (or maybe she never really knew them to begin with). She didn't care, she just made up the missing words:

> I'm going to dance with my Dolly
> with a hole in her stocking,
>
> and her knees kept a knocking,
>
> and her tail kept a rocking...

My Mother did not appreciate her lyrics.

I had a little baby doll named "Sweet Sue." Sweet Sue was my sleep companion, and I couldn't (or wouldn't) go to sleep without her. One day in the fall of the year—it must have been a Saturday—we were all out in the front yard raking up the leaves that had fallen from the two big red maple trees. Daddy, Mama, and Aunt Mary raked leaves while I played in them and caused trouble. My baby brother, Joe, was safe in his baby carriage while we were busy in the yard. Finally, we had gathered all the leaves in one gigantic pile so Daddy could rake them onto a tarp. From there, we would drag them to the garden, where they could rot into the soil.

That night, when it was time to go to bed, Sweet Sue was missing. First, I looked and looked all over the house, then I reported the loss to Mama, and she looked all over the house. Soon her patience ran out, and she began to raise the topic of my going to bed without my doll! It was not just that I needed Sweet Sue. It was that I was apprehensive about her being lost, knowing that I had given up without finding her.

As I began to express my thoughts and feelings loudly and continually, Aunt Mary took my hand and said, "Come on." We got the kerosene lantern out of the kitchen closet behind the wood stove, lighted it, and headed out to the yard where the leaf raking had taken place. Then, with Aunt Mary holding the lantern, I took the big rake and gradually unraked all the leaves until … There, at the bottom of the pile, we found Sweet Sue.

Sue was damp from the leaves and the ground (I was sure it was from her crying for me), but I took her directly to bed and slept soundly all night.

We always had a garden at our Plott Creek house. In the springtime, our up-the-road neighbor, Mr. Sorrells, would come down to our house with his mule and plow our garden. Then Daddy would start planting, mostly corn and beans. Then, everything else that came into his mind.

When Aunt Mary arrived, she became an avid part of the gardening scheme. When the next spring came, she showed up one afternoon with a flat of tiny green plants she had decided to add to the garden. They did not look like anything Daddy had ever set out. However, being a child, nothing was explained to me.

As they grew, you could hardly tell that they were blooming when they started growing some kind of small vegetable shaped like a tiny sharp-pointed baby's finger. As these little vegetables got bigger, they gradually turned from green to bright red. Aunt Mary finally told me they were called peppers, and I should not mess with them.

At the end of the summer, she pulled up the pepper plants and carried them all to the back porch. There she put on gloves and then pulled all of the little red peppers off of the limp plants. Then, using a needle and thread, Aunt Mary strung them in bunches which were then suspended on the porch. She told me they would keep for the winter.

I was inquisitive about these peppers. Mama and Daddy didn't ever eat any of them, only Aunt Mary. When we had something like dried beans to eat, Mary cut one of the peppers into very tiny pieces and ate them mixed with her beans. She told me not to touch them.

By this time in my life, I had learned that grown-ups were very selfish with the things they liked the most. While they pretended to be generous with children, they actually kept their favorite things for themselves. I observed adults telling children, "You would not like that," or "You're not old enough yet." This told me that the little red peppers must be delicious indeed.

One day soon after the stringing-up day, everyone was out in the garden digging the potatoes before the cold weather came. I was in the house by myself. I started looking out the window onto the porch and thinking about those beautiful little red peppers. After all, red was my favorite color, and that made them even more attractive. A decision was made.

I went out onto the porch, stood on a cane-bottom chair, and reached up to one of the strings of peppers. I pulled the bottom pepper off the string right over the knot and looked at it. I decided to put the whole thing in my mouth at one time so that if I didn't like it, there would not be a half-eaten part left as evidence. So, the bright red pepper, seeds and all, went into my mouth. I started chewing on it.

Aunt Mary was the first one to get back to the house when everyone heard my screaming. She later said that she knew exactly what had happened because no one could scream like that for any other reason. I had already spit everything out on the porch floor, so there was no lying about what had happened. She took me into the kitchen and got me to wash my mouth out, "real good." Then she started feeding me spoons full of sugar, which she told me to hold in my mouth as long as I could until all the sugar dissolved before getting the next one. She picked me up and carried me, "a million miles," she later swore, around and around the house while I cried and cried as well as I could with sugar in my mouth.

I never even looked at those peppers again, let alone touched one.

At last, Uncle Gudger came home from overseas, and Aunt Mary left our home. She and Uncle Gudger got a little house in Canton, where he had been hired to work in the accounting department of Champion Paper and Fibre Company. In time they had a baby girl they named Pollyanna, and I did not get to see my aunt as often as I once had.

As time passed, Uncle Gudger's mother, Mrs. Palmer, came to stay with them. She was a sweet old lady, and whenever we went to visit them, we also got to visit with her.

One Sunday, they were having dinner after church when, all of a sudden, Mrs. Palmer fell out of her chair and onto the floor. She couldn't talk or get up. Uncle Gudger and Aunt Mary got her off the floor and onto a bed in the bedroom. They called the doctor. That's what you did in those days before 911.

The doctor took one look at Mrs. Palmer and knew what had happened to her. After he finished his examination, he made the announcement: "She's had a very severe stroke. As you already know, she cannot speak, swallow, or manage herself in any physical way. In my opinion, there is no point in taking her to the hospital. They can't do anything for her. Besides, it is unlikely that she will live through the night. Her vital signs are diminishing."

After the doctor left, Aunt Mary turned to feed Pollyanna since she had been ignored for the past couple of hours. As Mary spooned baby food into Pollyanna, she got an idea. After the baby feeding was finished, she took some of Pollyanna's baby food, watered it down, and put it in a big basting syringe. Then Mary went to Mrs. Palmer, eased the basting syringe down her throat past where she could gag it back up, and fed her the watered-down baby food.

The next morning the doctor came back to see what had happened. Much to his surprise Mrs. Palmer was alive, and her vital signs had not changed for the worse. "Well," he commented, "she made it through the night, but she will never last out the week. I'll come back before the weekend unless you need to call me before then."

When he came on Friday, the doctor expressed surprise

that Mary had not called him during the week. Mrs. Palmer seemed to have stabilized. "Somehow," he wondered aloud to himself, "she is still going, but I wouldn't bet on her getting to the end of the month." Aunt Mary nodded, but day after day, kept on cleaning up Mrs. Palmer and feeding her watered-down baby food.

It was years later—the doctor was dead—when Mrs. Palmer finally died. Aunt Mary had kept her alive almost hour by hour through all of that time with her own invented critical nursing care.

Through those years of Mrs. Palmer's care, Aunt Mary had not been teaching school, and her credentials, without active renewal, had expired. So, she went back to school at Western Carolina Teachers' College to renew her certification. While doing that, Aunt Mary discovered something that had not existed back when she was in teachers' college for the first time: Special Education. She became so enamored with Special Education and the possibility of actually providing a school experience for children who had often grown up hidden at home that she continued on at Western Carolina and got her Master's Degree in Special Education.

In 1958, the first year self-contained Special Education classrooms came into being in Haywood County, Mary became a Special Education Teacher.

The class assigned to Aunt Mary that first year of her new career was what—in the terminology of the day—was called

"TMR," or "Trainable Mentally Retarded." This was to distinguish it from "EMR" or "Educable Mentally Retarded." Her students were considered to be on the lowest success end of the public education spectrum.

She loved it, and she was a natural. She had seven boys in her first class, all from ages thirteen to seventeen, and none of whom had ever been to school before. Even the thirteen-year-old was heavier than she was, but she could pick any of them up if she needed to. Mary already knew five of the boys from knowing their families in a small town.

One Sunday, we had Uncle Gudger and Aunt Mary for Sunday dinner after church. We had about finished eating a meal, during which most of the conversation had been Aunt Mary's telling us more and more about "her boys" and her classroom adventures. When there was a pause in the conversation, Daddy asked her: "Mary, I don't see how you can do that! I mean, those boys are bigger than you. I doubt you can understand a word most of them are trying to say. Why, they can't do hardly anything. I know some of them from knowing their families."

She smiled and started, "There's nothing to it, Joe. You see, every one of my boys can tell me what he needs if I just have the patience to listen until I understand them. Mrs. Palmer couldn't do that. Every one of my boys can actually feed himself by now. Mrs. Palmer couldn't do that. Three of my boys already learned to take themselves to the bathroom, and every one of them can now wash their hands. Mrs. Palmer couldn't do that. And they can all manage their own clothing. The boys take their coats off and on in the mornings and afternoons. Mrs. Palmer couldn't do that."

As I listened to Mary's answer, I realized that, far from the tragedy we all believed her burden of care for Mrs. Palmer had been, it had instead been the preparation for her becoming an absolutely splendid Special Education teacher.

One day, I—now a driving teenager—was sent by Mama to take Aunt Mary something after the end of the school day. "She'll still be at school if you hurry," she prompted. I drove to the school to find that all of her students had been picked up by their mothers except one. His mother was there, but he was not quite ready to go.

As his mother watched patiently, Aunt Mary explained, "See, he's my alignment expert. He needs to be sure the classroom is in order before he can go home." While we watched, this big boy gently pushed all the tables and chairs until they were perfectly in line with the black and white tiles on the floor. He then moved around the room straightening and lining up everything else until he was satisfied, then he was happy to go home with his mother.

He put on his own coat. Then, in a moment of surprise, he jumped in the air and grabbed Aunt Mary around the neck with such surprising force that they both fell to the floor. Both stood, laughing. "I love you, Miz Palmer," his voice was clearly understandable, "You're just like me!"

Once he and his mother were gone and I had delivered the package from Mama, Aunt Mary told me, "What just then happened is the reward for doing this ... he just gave me the best prize any teacher will ever expect to get."

Aunt Mary continued to teach year after year until her North Carolina driver's license said that she was seventy years old. In no way was she ready to retire, but the teaching rules of North Carolina said that seventy was the retirement age.

One day not so long after that, Aunt Mary and Uncle Gudger were at home. He was watching a ball game on television, and she was scurrying around the house as usual. All of a sudden, she came trotting through the living room and commented to him, "I'm tired, Gudger. I need to go and lie down for a little bit." She disappeared into the bedroom. Gudger immediately realized that, in all of their life together, he had never heard her utter those words, "I'm tired." By the time he made it to the bedroom, she was gone.

By now, I was an adult in my middle thirties. My wife and I traveled up to the mountains for the funeral. The church was packed; Aunt Mary was the kind of person who instantly knew everyone she met.

When the service was over, we proceeded to the cemetery. She was being buried at Crabtree on the way to Iron Duff, where she and my Daddy had grown up. We finished at the cemetery but, before leaving, Uncle Gudger walked over to the funeral home car in which he had ridden to the cemetery, reached in the back seat, and took something out. What he removed from the car was a blue and white sports pennant that said, "UNC."

Even though he grew up in the tiny mountain community of Cataloochee (now inside the Great Smoky Mountains National Park), Uncle Gudger had gone to the University of North Carolina in Chapel Hill. He and Mary were both dedicated UNC sports fans. He took the blue and white pennant over to her grave that had just been filled, and stuck it upright in the middle of the flower arrangements that had been placed on top, then dusted his hands together and walked away.

"Isn't that sweet," I heard someone say. "Mary did love UNC, basketball especially."

With his usual droll humor, Uncle Gudger responded, "Nothing sweet about it. It's purely practical. You see, Mary knows everybody in this cemetery. I know where we buried her today, but whenever I come back out here, there's no telling who she might have run off to see. I reckon she might take this little flag with her. That way, I will know where to find her when I come back out here." For years after that, everyone who knew Mary always moved the pennant around whenever they were at the cemetery so that Gudger would know for sure that dear friends were actively remembering her.

Pollyanna had married Jim, a blinded Vietnam War veteran, and they lived a few miles from Uncle Gudger. Gudger lived alone in the same little house he and Mary had bought after he got home from overseas. He was totally independent.

When he was ninety-nine years old, his driver's license expired, and he went down to the DMV to get it renewed. He explained to them, "I don't drive anymore. I keep my Dodge in the garage. I go out there and start it every day, just to be sure it will run if I need it. I won't drive it unless there is an emergency." They renewed his driver's license for five more years.

Uncle Gudger died when he was 103 years old. I had been with him at the Cataloochee Reunion a few weeks before, and he seemed as well as he had been when he was 102. Then one day, I received a message from Pollyanna, "I think Gudger's getting ready to leave," was all it said. He died three days later.

A half-dozen years later, both Polly and her husband, Jim, were killed in an automobile accident. Authorities surmised that she, the driver, had a "medical incident." Perhaps she departed this life the same way Aunt Mary did.

Sometimes I lapse into going far too long without actively remembering all of them. Then, one evening, a reminder will come. We live on Ocracoke Island inside the boundaries of Cape Hatteras National Seashore, a park that is designated as a darkness preservation park. It is a place with a gigantic night sky that, free from light pollution, is home to heavenly displays, from millions of stars to a gigantic moon to the long sweep of the Milky Way.

On some of those clear nights when we are stargazing, a sudden gift occurs: a huge meteorite will trace its shooting-star path across the sky, and Aunt Mary is back! "Do you know that there is a star in the sky for every baby ever to be born on this earth?" And now, I know for sure that Aunt Mary has found hers.

Chapter Two

Grandmother Walker

MY FATHER'S MOTHER (WHO WAS ALSO AUNT MARY'S MOTHER)
died in 1943, six months before I was born. Since his father
had died in 1920, I never knew my grandparents on the pa-
ternal side of the family. So, whenever I think of grandparents,
I automatically picture my mother's parents, Grandmother
and Granddaddy Walker.

You could have blindfolded me at age eight and carried
me into their house in the middle of the night, and I could
have told you where we were just from the smell. The house
smelled like raw wood that had never been painted or finished in any way. It smelled like wood smoke from both the
wood heater in the front room and the wood cookstove in the
kitchen. It smelled like frying pork from frying pork for a hundred years. It smelled of mildew from the excessive rainfall of
the North Carolina mountains. And it smelled like snuff spit.
Hidden in every room, sometimes beside the corner of a chair

leg, sometimes on the windowsill, you could find my Grand-mother's snuff spit cans.

She dipped Dental Scotch Snuff constantly, and the snuff smell barely seasoned all the other sweet smells of that place so dear to me.

Many times in the summer of my growing up years, Mama would announce to me: "Guess what? Your Grand-mother wants you to come and spend a week with her." I thought the invitation was because I was such a precious child. It never occurred to me that my absence would give my mother a blessed week, having only my little brother, Joe, to follow about the house and yard. Breakfast was one of my favorite times of the day when I got to spend time there. Granddaddy Walker would lie in bed in the mornings until Grandmother called to tell him it was time to eat. So, if I got up earlier than that, I got to be with Grandmother by myself first thing in the morning.

We would go out to the spring behind the house and carry water into the kitchen for the day. Then we would walk up to the barn, and I would loaf around while she milked the cow. All this time, while we milked (and loafed), came back to the house, strained the milk, skimmed the cream, and put it all into the spring house, the woodstove would be heating up for cooking breakfast.

By now, the stove was hot, and we would put the coffee

on to perk. While the coffee perked, Grandmother would mix up the biscuit dough in her big wooden bowl, cut the biscuits out, arrange them in the blackened pan, and slide the pan into the oven just as she determined that the temperature was exactly right by holding her hand in the open oven door for a moment.

When Granddaddy smelled the coffee, he was likely to get up and come into the kitchen before being called. Grandmother would pour him a big cup of coffee and spoon sugar and cream into it. He would pick up the cup and saucer, tip some coffee over into the saucer so it could cool, and drink the first sips out of the saucer.

While the biscuits were baking, Grandmother fried sausage patties she had made from the hog they had killed back in the wintertime. No sausage in my life since then has ever had either the taste or the perfect tenderness of hers. Once cooked to her satisfaction, the sausage was lifted out and forked onto a plate. Fresh eggs were then broken into the sausage grease to scramble so that they were perfectly done just as the biscuits came out of the oven.

Then we ate, and ate, and ate. Eggs and sausage were first. Biscuits with butter and jelly were next (and then more biscuits with more butter and jelly). We were set for most of the day after that.

After breakfast was over, I would help Grandmother scrape anything that was left on the plates into the slop bucket that was always waiting by the back door to receive pig offerings. Our last breakfast task was to wash and dry the dishes and put them away for the next meal.

What came after that was the most interesting ritual of the morning: time for Granddaddy's morning shave.

Grandmother would heat water in the tea kettle on the stove while Granddaddy pulled out a tall wooden stool, sat on the stool, and lowered the top of his bib overalls. Grandmother would pour hot water over a towel, wring out the towel, and place the hot, wet towel on Granddaddy's face while he leaned back on the stool.

As the hot towel softened his beard, she would get out her straight razor, open it up, and strop it on the leather razor strap that hung from the windowsill beside the wood stove. When it was satisfactory, she dribbled a little bit of hot water into her shaving mug and, with her shaving brush, whipped up a good mound of hot lather.

Now the towel came off Granddaddy's face, and the lather was brushed on, down from his ears, over his cheeks, under his chin, and under his nose.

Then the straight razor went into action. Grandmother carefully held it with her little finger controlling the back end, delicately shaving everywhere the lather had covered. Granddaddy never moved through all of this. In no time, she finished by washing the rest of the suds off his face, and he was ready to button up the bib on his overalls and face the day. I never tired of watching the morning shave.

We did all kinds of things when I was at Grandmother's house. Since it was always summertime when I got to spend the week there, it was always garden time. Grandmother's garden was huge. She could never cut down from the days when she was feeding nine children as well as Granddaddy and herself. She kept raising large amounts of produce so that whenever company came from out of town, she could send them home with potatoes, onions, tomatoes, corn, and beans. Her garden gifts reflected the growing season: whatever was ready to harvest at the time. She also kept canning much more than was needed for the same reason. I loved to work with her in the garden, where the dirt warmed my bare feet, and I could get as dirty as I wanted.

Other special treats happened when I was there. My grandparents lived on a rural mail route. The mailman came every day but Sunday. The mailbox was not at the house but rather was down beside the paved county road. To get to it, you had to walk a couple of hundred yards down a path between the creek and a field. You could, however, see the mailbox from the front porch of the house so you could tell from the little flag whether the mailman had been there for the day. It was not the mail, though, that interested me.

Two other services loosely followed the mail route, each coming one day a week. One was Grady Hunnycut's Store on

Wheels, and the other was the Haywood County Public Library Bookmobile.

The Store on Wheels was an old, superannuated school bus that Grady Hunnycut had bought from the county when the school thought it needed to be replaced. He had overhauled it mechanically, taken out the seats, and painted the bus inside and out. One day each week, we would see the Store on Wheels coming down the road a little while after the mailman had come.

Grady Hunnycut himself drove the bus and ran the store. A cold drink box stood just inside the door, and close by were shelves of cigarettes, snuff, cigars, chewing tobacco, and pipe tobacco. Other shelves displayed penny candy, nickel candy bars, and other snacks, including a big jar of pickles and another big jar of pickled eggs. Beyond that, the bus held shelves with sewing notions, fabric, pots and pans, hardware, and tools. The store, as Grady said, held "about one of everything." If he did not have your requested item, he would write your wish on his list, and he would bring it from town the following week. (Many people, like my grandparents, did not drive or have cars.)

On some days, especially after we had worked in the garden all morning, Grandmother and I would walk down to the road after the mailman passed and wait for the Store on Wheels. When it stopped, and Grady Hunnycut opened the door, we would climb inside the bus where I could look at everything. Grandmother would buy some Dental Scotch Snuff and get me some peppermint candy sticks. I thought that Grady Hunnycut must be a rich man to have all the stuff in the Store on Wheels.

Even though we only sometimes visited the Store on Wheels, we never missed the days on which the Bookmobile came. In the summertime, when school was out, the library wanted to promote reading by children. So, in the summertime, you could check out ten books instead of the limit of three that was imposed during the school year. I always had plenty to read at Grandmother's house. She also loved to read. On days when the work was done, the two of us might sit side by side on the porch and read during the afternoon while supper was simmering on the stove.

One morning, when I was spending the week, I was still in bed when there was a sharp knock at the door of the house. I sat up in bed to listen while Grandmother went to the door. She did not step out onto the porch. Whoever was there did not come inside, so I could only hear her side of the conversation.

"When did she die?

"Well, she had been sick for a long time.

"She was eighty-nine, her last birthday as I remember...

"Oh, course. I'll be down there in a little bit."

As the door closed and she headed back to the kitchen, I came out of the room where I slept. I knew she would tell

Granddaddy what was going on, and I could listen in. Then I would know also.

"Who was that this early in the morning?" Granddaddy asked as we both walked into the kitchen, where she was drinking coffee while the biscuits were baking.

"That was Robert from down the road. Old Miz Fox, his mama, died last night."

Granddaddy nodded. "Well, she's been sick a long time, don't you know. I guess her time just came. What did he want?"

"Oh," she started, "He just came to ask me if I might come down there and lay her out." I was totally baffled. What did 'laying out' mean? It sounded like fighting to me. I had never seen Grandmother fight with somebody, but as tiny and tough as she was, I figured that, if she had to, she could lay somebody out.

"I'm going to go on down there," she said to Granddaddy.

There were well over a dozen grandchildren by this time, but, as far as Granddaddy was concerned, we only had one of two names. We were either *the boy* or *the girl*. He said to Grandmother, "Do you want me to keep the boy?"

"No," she answered, "I'm going to take Donald with me." She told me to get my clothes on while she got ready. By the time I was back in the kitchen, Grandmother had changed her clothes. She had with her a small cardboard-looking suitcase. We told Granddaddy we'd be back "after a while," and we headed out the door.

The old, dusty road that the paved county road had replaced still ran from farm to farm even though it was abandoned and fenced off by various landowners as it crossed their property. We walked down this old road since it would go by the Fox's house on the way to Ferguson's Store. We went through the gate that I knew marked the end of my grandparent's land, and then over the next hill, we arrived at the Fox place.

The house was big. It was two stories with a first-floor porch that ran around three sides of the house. We walked up the steps to the porch, and Grandmother knocked on the front door. Robert came to the door.

"Silas Smart made the coffin," Robert said to us when he opened the door. "He put it out on the back porch."

"Well," Grandmother started, "You and your wife go on down to the store and hang around there for maybe a long hour. By that time, I ought to be all finished." Robert nodded. By this time, his wife had joined us on the porch. Then Grandmother asked, "Would you happen to have a couple of tow sacks we could have?"

"Well, I am sure that we do. What do you need them for?"

"You see, I brought my grandson, Donald, here. If you don't mind, I thought he could pick up *warnets* down at that big tree while I am working inside the house." (I knew that "warnets" was what my Grandmother called walnuts. This was part of her vocabulary.)

Robert's wife disappeared into the house and came back out in a few minutes with two tow sacks that she handed to me. "Help yourself," she smiled at me. "Gather up all them nuts that you want. We don't do nothing with 'em."

Grandmother told them, "Goodbye," as they headed down toward the store, and I took my sacks and headed down to the "warnet" tree. Grandmother took her little suitcase and disappeared into the house.

I picked up walnuts for a total of about ten minutes. Then a terrible and acute curiosity virus hit me: I had to know what was going on inside that house.

Very carefully, I walked up through the yard and climbed the steps to the big porch. First of all, I went to the right-hand end, around the right corner of the house. When I peeked into the window there, all I saw was the empty kitchen. Nothing going on in there. Then I came back around to the windows beside the front door. They led into the front room of the house, and there was no one in there. Frustrated, I tip-toed down to the far end of the porch and around the other corner of the house. This time I hit pay dirt!

As I peered through the window, I could see Grandmother's back as she stood facing a big bed. Near the foot of the bed, I could see strangely white feet. At the head of the bed, I watched Grandmother as she brushed out dead Mrs.

Fox's long white hair. I was mesmerized as I watched her braid the long, brushed-out hair and coil it up onto Mrs. Fox's head, where she fastened it with several combs. Then I watched as she bathed Mrs. Fox's face. Now I knew what "laying out" was. I also knew that if I got caught, I would be next in line.

Just then, the clouds shifted, and the sun came out on my back. In that instant, I saw my shadow projected on the far wall of the bedroom. Without thinking, I dived off the porch and ran back down through the yard to where I had left the sacks on the ground. For the next long minutes, you would never have seen anyone pick up walnuts as fast as I did. In no time, both tow sacks were full to the top.

In a little while, I heard the front door open and close. When I looked up there, Grandmother was coming down the front steps from the big porch. She walked down through the yard and looked at my filled sacks of walnuts. "You've probably been wondering what I was doing in there," she started.

"NO!" I insisted. "I hadn't even thought about it. I've been busy sacking up walnuts."

She laughed. "Well, come on with me anyway. Let me show you what I was doing before Robert and his wife get back from the store."

She led me by the hand like she knew I was nervous, up to the porch and in the front door. We were now in the front room of the big house. I remembered that Robert had told

Grandmother that Silas Smart, who built the coffin, had put it on the back porch. I also knew I had seen her working in one of the bedrooms. Grandmother was not a large woman, but she was strong. The six-sided pine coffin was resting on two chairs against the front room wall. As we walked up to it, I saw old Mrs. Fox, all dressed in a blue dress and with her hair neatly braided and put up, resting there in the coffin. She was so calm and beautiful. There was nothing scary about it in this world.

Grandmother pushed a loose hair off Mrs. Fox's face and said to me, "She's been sick and suffering for a long time. She deserves to get to be dead."

About that time, Robert and his wife arrived back at the house. They looked at Mrs. Fox and told Grandmother she had done a respectful job. Robert thanked her and said, "How much do I owe you?"

"It was an honor for you to ask me, Robert. You do not owe me one thing. Besides, I got a bonus today because my grandson, Donald, got to come with me. He got two sacks of warnets picked up. If it's alright with you, you might keep one sack and let us take the other one home with us. There's a lot of warnets still to come off of that tree."

Robert thanked me. I fetched the heavier sack of walnuts for them, and Grandmother slung the other bag over her shoulder to carry it back home with us. We started back up the road.

As we walked along, I remember reaching up and taking my Grandmother by the hand. I thought about all that had happened that day and began to realize: my Grandmother was one of the most important people in this world. I knew that people came to see my Granddaddy when they needed a cow dehorned or some bees robbed. They came to see my Daddy if they needed to talk about borrowing money from the bank. They came to see my Mama if they were having trouble with one of their children (whom she had usually taught in elementary school). But it was my Grandmother people came to see when someone they loved died. They could ask her to prepare the deceased for their final rest through eternity. Who could be more important than that?

In the years that followed, I never tired of time spent at Grandmother and Granddaddy's house. By the time I went off to college, I had come to realize that visiting with them was like seeing a museum of my own personal history; they told me who I was and from whom I had come.

Grandmother did not enjoy good health as she aged. She was dogged by both cancer and a series of heart attacks that finally took her from this life when she was only seventy-seven years old.

When she died, I was grown up and in my thirties. I well remember making the trip back home with my family for her funeral. What I remember most is going up into town to

Garrett's Funeral Home with just my mother and father a little bit before general visitation started in the evening.

As we went into the funeral home, we were met by Mr. Ernest Edwards of the Funeral Home. "We have two people here this evening," he said to all of us. "Mrs. Walker is in the reception room on this side," he pointed with his hand toward the open door of one of the large viewing rooms.

We walked into the room, and I escorted my mother up to the open casket. There was a woman in the silver metallic casket. The woman looked like she had spent the afternoon at the beauty parlor. Her hair looked like she had had a permanent, and she was wearing rouge and lipstick. Her glasses lay folded in her hands.

My Grandmother had never been inside a beauty parlor and never even owned a tube of lipstick in her life. I had also never seen her not wearing her glasses. My first thought was that we had come into the wrong room, and this was not my Grandmother.

Of course, it was her, and, of course, I actually knew that all the time. But, in that very moment, I remembered our day at the Fox's house and wished in my heart that there could have been someone to care for her as she had cared for Mrs. Fox. Didn't Grandmother Walker deserve someone to lay her out, bathe her, dress her in a suitable outfit, and braid her hair? Surely, if asked, a handy neighbor would make her a six-sided coffin of heart pine, a coffin with rope handles on the sides, and cut nails to secure the lid on the top. I wished she could have spent this night in the front room of her own house while neighbors and relatives came to bring food and tell stories. After all, she had lived out her life admirably. Her days had been productive, her lot hard, and she deserved to rest with the dead.

Chapter Three

Mrs. Ledbetter

WHEN I WAS SIX YEARS OLD, I started school at Hazelwood Elementary School right next to Waynesville, North Carolina. Mr. Lawrence Leatherwood was the school principal, and my first-grade teacher was Mrs. Annie Ledbetter.

Mrs. Ledbetter and her husband, called 'Ott' (maybe a nickname for Arthur), lived only about three blocks from the school. Ott was one of the owners of the big hardware in Hazelwood. The Ledbetters had no children, and for years her "children" were always the children whom she taught. Since we did not have public school kindergarten, Mrs. Ledbetter was our first experience in the world of childhood education.

My Mama was thrilled with Mrs. Ledbetter being my teacher. "She's the best first-grade teacher there is," she told Daddy. Everybody in Waynesville and Hazelwood knew one another and remembered all of the gossip about reputations as well. This was not just my Mama's opinion; it was regarded as a community fact.

This year Mrs. Ledbetter's class was everyone whose last name started with the letters 'A' through 'Gr,' Charlotte Abernathy through Lady Ruth Greene. Another reason we knew that Mrs. Ledbetter was the best first-grade teacher in the school was that, all out of alphabetic order, Harris Prevost was also in her room. The biggest employer in town was Harris' grandfather at Unagusta Furniture, so, given this fact, his mother got to choose his teacher. Back then, the world was fair!

Mrs. Ledbetter was a jolly, substantially-built woman. I am sure that pants never touched her legs. She had five teacher dresses that she wore in the same order each week: there was the Monday dress, the Tuesday dress, the Wednesday dress, the Thursday dress, and the Friday dress. The Monday dress was a dull gray-brown color. After Monday, Miss Annie's dresses got brighter each day of the week. If she had worn them in chromatic order, we would have learned our colors right off.

Our favorite dress was the Friday dress. Friday was red dress day. The red dress was the color that fire trucks are supposed to be: just a bit darker than the brightest red. It was some sort of double-knit material and was stretchy so that it could go in and out with the tide as needed.

The red dress also had very narrow piping stripes that ran up and down and back and forth, dividing it into little oblong blocks of red. One Friday early in the year, we came to school, and she was wearing the red dress. As soon as Harris got there,

44

he looked up at her and smiled. "Oh, Mrs. Ledbetter," he started. "I just love it when you wear that dress. It makes you look like a beautiful big brick building." Before anyone else got a chance to react, Mrs. Ledbetter started laughing. She laughed and laughed and laughed so hard that she cried, and tears ran down her face. It was right then that, having heard about some of the other first-grade teachers, I knew that we were very lucky; we were the class that had the teacher who knew how to laugh.

Laughing was very important to Mrs. Ledbetter. She often laughed when we did not know what was funny. Sometimes we asked her, "What was so funny about that?"

She would reply, "Oh, you don't just laugh about things because something is funny. You laugh to get yourself back from somewhere else to being yourself again." We did not understand this at all, but we remembered it and thought about it.

Back in those days, boys routinely carried in their pockets many things that are prohibited today: in addition to marbles and string, we always had matches and pocketknives. After all, who knew when you or someone around you might need a match or a pocketknife? Knife trading was an art practiced by some of the rougher boys, and the only rule I remember about knives in school was "no knife trading."

Every day that the weather was reasonable, we had recess.

Recess was not physical education. It was time to "let off steam." We were turned outside for a set period, and—with playground equipment like giant swings and sliding boards—we simply did what we wanted until the teachers called us back. Sometimes, if the teacher needed to catch up on something, they did not even go out with us. We were just left on our own.

One of the boys' favorite games, especially during those unsupervised times, was called "playing stretch." It required knives. You stood facing your opponent, both of you holding open pocket knives. Then the first person threw their knife down to stick the blade into the ground as close to the outside of one of their opponent's feet as possible. That person then had to move this foot out until it touched the knife. He then threw his knife beside one of his opponent's feet, and so the "stretch" began and continued until someone had stretched so far that they fell down and lost the game.

In those days, many children—both boys and girls—went to school with bare feet until the weather got so cold that it was not possible. This meant that sometimes the "stretch" games were played by boys with bare feet.

One of those days, Tommy Conard and Aldean Conner began playing "stretch," and Tommy was barefoot. We were all gathered around, watching as they already had their legs widely spread. It was Aldean's turn to throw his knife into the ground beside Tommy's foot. He threw the knife, but his aim was a little bit off, and it stuck right into the edge of Tommy's foot, just behind his little toe.

Tommy squalled. "Oh, oh, oh, oh, oh ..." and kept on wailing. We decided it was time for recess to be over, and we all headed back into the school building with Tommy limping along behind ... trailing blood from his foot.

As soon as we were inside, Mrs. Ledbetter saw what had happened. She looked at Tommy and started laughing. He got mad. "Why are you laughing? It's not funny."

Mrs. Ledbetter kept laughing. "Tommy," she said, "In the whole scheme of things, it *is* funny. Besides, if you want it to stop hurting, then you should laugh. That will take care of it. Laugh at what happened. Laugh because you can't go back and undo it. Laugh because, in twenty years, you will look back and tell about it, and everyone will laugh. Laugh because Mr. Ledbetter will laugh when I tell him about this tonight. Laughing cures things. Laughter brings us back from being someone else to being ourselves again."

Tommy started laughing. As soon as he started laughing, Aldean, who was sure he was in terrible trouble, started laughing. When the two of them started laughing, the rest of us started laughing. We laughed and laughed. Pretty soon, Tommy wasn't even thinking about his foot hurting. Finally, Mrs. Ledbetter said, "Now go in the bathroom and wash it so we can get back to arithmetic." Everything was settled and over with.

As the year went on, every time something upset someone,

Mrs. Ledbetter's solution was for us to laugh about it.

Our room was at the end of the building, close to the auditorium. The lunch room was in the next building at the far end. To go to lunch, we had to go down the hall and out the door. Then there was a covered walk about thirty feet long that took us into the lunchroom. In the wintertime, when it got below freezing, we always had to wear our coats to go to lunch.

One day in the winter, we were finishing our lunch when Harold Allen got an idea. "When you finish your milk," he told several of us, "Go over to the fountain and fill your milk carton up with water and keep it like you haven't finished it yet. Then when we go back across to the other building, let's pour the water beside the sidewalk where it slopes downhill. That way, it can freeze and make an ice slide for us to play on later."

We did it. For days after that, one half-pint at a time, water was poured beside the sidewalk. Gradually, there grew a frozen slide of ice from the sidewalk down the hill to the play-ground. The ice was a pale blue-white from the final dregs of milk left in our cartons when we filled them with water. Now, at recess and after school, we could slide down the hill. We were very proud of ourselves.

One day several of us boys were sliding down the ice at recess when Shirley Clark stuck her nose in our business. She, a girl, actually wanted to slide down the ice like we did. Since she was by this time taller than most of us, we had no choice but to get out of the way and let her do it.

She started out sliding down the hill like we did, but part of the way down, her body rotated, and she tumbled over and ended up face-down on the ice at the bottom. When she stood, we could see that she had blood around her mouth. She had a fairly good busted lip. And Shirley was crying.

We all ran inside the building, thinking we would be blamed for the accident. When we got to our room, Mrs. Ledbetter looked up at the clock noticing that we had returned from recess before we were even called. Then Shirley arrived, with blood dripping.

Mrs. Ledbetter checked to be sure Shirley had not knocked a tooth loose, and then she started laughing! "Now, Shirley," she began. "You know by now that laughing takes away the pain when you get hurt a little bit. You're not hurt very much, so a lot of laughing ought to take care of it."

Shirley started laughing, and then she asked the rest of us, "Why aren't you all laughing? You know that it feels better when everybody laughs" We had been afraid that she might get mad if we laughed, but now, with her encouragement, we all laughed and laughed. We knew that when Mrs. Ledbetter got home that night, she would tell Mr. Ledbetter about what had happened, and they would both laugh. I knew that when I got home that night, I would tell everyone at our house about it, and we would all laugh. Mrs. Ledbetter was right: laughing was a good way to take away the pain and make everyone feel better. It sure was better than crying.

As the year rolled along, we got a new student in our class. Her name was Carol White, and Mrs. Ledbetter told us that she and her mother had moved to town from Florida. Even though she was not one of the "A's through Gr's," she was put in our class because we had one student fewer than the other first-grade classes. When I told Mama about this, and she heard that Carol and her mother had moved from Florida, she told me that this meant Carol was from a broken home. I had no idea what this meant. Maybe something in their house didn't work because it was broken. I didn't understand how Mama knew this since we didn't even know where they lived.

The first day that she was in our class, my best friend, Harris, and I each decided we were in love with her. How we each knew that the other of us was in love, I cannot remember, but it was quickly clear that we were in serious competition for her attention. As the day went on, neither Harris nor I made much progress in getting her attention, and we were mutually frustrated.

The next day this new Carol paid us as little attention as she had the first day, and both Harris and I were getting desperate. That afternoon, though, we got our chance to go for the win. Mrs. Ledbetter announced that we would have art time and get to do some tempera painting. We loved to do this, and she had excellent equipment that must have been made for her by Mr. Ledbetter.

We had large wooden double-sided easels. They opened on hinges at the top, and two people could use them, with one standing on each side. There was a clamp at the top to hold your paper in place and a gutter-like shelf along the bottom that held about nine jars of tempera paint. We had red, orange, yellow, green, blue, purple, brown, black, and white. The paint was in screw-top jars, so we opened them up to paint and then closed them back up to save them for the next art period. So, each jar had quite a bit of paint in it.

We were all painting away, each person deciding on this day what our subject would be when Mrs. Ledbetter announced. "Boys and girls, I need to go down to the store-room and get us some more paper ... we are running out. While I am gone ... Donald and Harris ... you boys behave!"

Harris and I wondered at times like this what happened to the rest of our class. We were always the only ones who were named whenever Mrs. Ledbetter issued a warning of any kind. Maybe we were just her favorite students!

As soon as she went out the door, Harris and I each got the same idea at the same time. We didn't need to communicate with each other. Each of us just knew what we had to do. If we were going to win Carol's attention and her heart, one of us had to be the first one to mark her. So, each of us dipped our brush in the paint color we knew she would love, and we started chasing her around the room. There were about a dozen of the big wooden easels scattered around the classroom with two painters assigned to each. This made a nice maze through which we were chasing Carol, and she was good at running from and avoiding us.

Who knows who did it? There was so much excitement and movement now as our classmates got into the contest and were cheering for one of the three of us that it might have been anyone … but, someone hit one of the easels in the process of running and over it went, crashing to the floor and dumping eighteen jars of tempera paint all over the floor just as Mrs. Ledbetter came back into the room. Everyone stood frozen, staring at Harris and at me, their stares focusing Mrs. Ledbetter's vision directly toward the two of us.

She started laughing, but to the two of us, it didn't seem very funny. The rest of the class started laughing. Carol was laughing harder than anyone. Harris and I tried to laugh, but it didn't come out easily. "Wait until I tell Mr. Ledbetter about this day … he is going to laugh his head off. Now, Harris and Donald, you may proceed to clean up the paint." She gave us rags and a bucket for water, and we spent most of the rest of the afternoon scrubbing the tempera paint off the floor.

When we finished our clean-up job, there was only about a half-hour left before the bell rang. Harris and I started to go back to our desks once we had thrown the cleaning rags away as Mrs. Ledbetter told us, but she stopped us. "Now, boys," she said, "there's just enough time for you to be punished."

"Punished!" we both said together. "We got punished by cleaning up all the paint."

"No," she said. "That was not punishment. That was just cleaning up the paint. You boys didn't mean to spill that paint. It was an accident that simply had to be cleaned up. You are being punished because when I left the room, I told both of you by name to behave, and you did not do what I told you."

She brought us up to the blackboard and drew two chalk circles on the board just about the height of our faces. "Now," she directed us, "you boys stand there with your noses touching the blackboard inside that ring for fifteen minutes, and think about listening the next time I tell you to behave. When I get home tonight and tell Mr. Ledbetter about this, he and I are both going to laugh, but right now, there will not be any laughing." Harris and I behaved better after that.

Neither one of us won the affection of Carol White, not because we did not try, but because she did not stay at Hazelwood School for more than a month at most. One day she was gone, and Mrs. Ledbetter told us that she and her mother had gone back to Florida. That was the last that we saw of her.

The year rolled on, and every time something went out of order in her room, Mrs. Ledbetter led us in the process of our laughing ourselves back to where we needed to be. It was a practice that I have remembered to this day, and I continue to make myself laugh at mistakes ranging from banking errors to smashed fingers. It works remarkably well.

One day a couple of months later, we were in class when Mrs. Ledbetter needed to go down the hall to the office for some sort of errand. She told all of us to behave while she was gone, and we continued to work on our arithmetic after she had left the room. When she came back into the room, we met a different teacher from the Mrs. Ledbetter we had come to know all year. She was crying.

The entire room was totally silent. We had never seen Mrs. Ledbetter even have a sad face, let alone a face with tears coming from her eyes. She pulled tissues from the box on her desk and wiped her nose. We all stared at her in confusion.

"Boys and girls," she started, "When I went down to the office, I am afraid that I learned some very bad news. You all remember Carol, who was in our class for just a few weeks? Well, she and her mother moved back to Florida. They moved into a house there, and two days ago, the house caught fire in the night. They were both asleep and didn't know the house was on fire. I am afraid that Carol and her mother both died in the fire."

We all just sat there. No one said anything. None of us had ever known of someone our age to die in any way, and this way seemed more terrible than we could imagine. "She died of what was called 'smoke inhalation,' not actually the fire itself but the smoke that she breathed in while she slept. The fireman got her out of the burning house, but it was too late." We all just sat there and watched Mrs. Ledbetter wipe the tears from her face over and over again.

Suddenly we heard a strange sound coming from the back of the room. It sounded like laughter. It *was* laughter. Eddie Birchfield was laughing. Before thinking about what she was saying, Mrs. Ledbetter asked, "Why are you laughing, Eddie? This is not funny."

"I just remember that day when Donald and Harris chased her around the room and knocked paint all over the room. If we hadn't had Carol in our class, that would not have ever happened. You taught us to laugh to make the pain go away, and so that is what I was doing."

Then Mrs. Ledbetter got a huge smile on her face, and she started to laugh. "You are right, Eddie. We must all laugh. We would not miss someone when they are gone if we had not had happy and funny times with them. Donald, why don't you tell us all your version of what you and Harris were trying to do on that day and how it all turned out for you."

Before it was all over, Mrs. Ledbetter had me draw rings on the blackboard, and we all went up there to see what it felt like when Harris and I had been punished for not behaving. We told as many funny stories as we could about Carol and all the things we remembered about her. We laughed until we got back to being ourselves again.

I shall never forget that day. When my wife, Merle, died in 2017, I sat alone in our bedroom and cried very loudly for some long minutes. Then Mrs. Ledbetter spoke to me out of a world beyond the present, and I started laughing. I remembered and laughed and remembered and laughed until I got back to being myself again. Then I once again thanked that great first-grade teacher for teaching us much more than arithmetic.

Chapter Four

The Goat Man

I WAS ABOUT TEN YEARS OLD, and we still lived on Plott Creek Road when Daddy came home early and in a big hurry one afternoon. "Come on," he said as soon as he entered the door. "We've got to go right now... The Goat Man is coming!"

None of us, including Mama, had any idea what he was talking about. What was a Goat Man, and why did Daddy want us to see it?

Mama looked at Daddy with questions in her eyes. "They say he comes through here every two or three years. We've never seen him before. He's supposed to be spending the night down across from Ben Sloan's house.

"Joe," Mama started, "You have got on your new suit. Don't you think you ought to change into some old clothes before we do this? You've only had that suit for a week."

"We don't have time," was Daddy's answer. "We need to get down there so we won't miss anything."

My brother, Joe, and I just stood and listened. We had never seen our Daddy get this excited about anything before. Whatever the Goat Man was, it must be something worth rushing to see. He and I were ready.

We all got in the car, and Daddy backed out of the driveway. He drove down Plott Creek Road to where it ended just below our house at Eagle's Nest Road. We turned left and drove down that road beside Richland Creek. Way before we got near Ben Sloan's house, we could all tell that something unusual was going on.

First of all, there were cars pulled off to the edge on both sides of the road, and people were walking from their parked cars down the road ahead of us. Daddy found an open space and pulled our car off on the edge.

"Look at that!" Mama exclaimed, and we looked toward where she was pointing to see a column of thick black smoke coming up over the trees beside the road ahead of us. There was also a never-smelled-before combination of terrible odors in the air. We followed as Daddy quickly led the way, following all the other people.

Sure enough, directly across the road from Ben Sloan's house, there was a long empty field that backed up to Richland Creek. People were gathered in a large circle around an old wagon, about twenty-five or thirty goats, and the fire burning with pieces of old truck tire smoking on top of it, all managed by a rough-looking old man with a long beard. The man wore overalls and a denim coat that looked greasy, like it had never been washed in its life. He was the Goat Man!

He was pretty much ignoring the crowd as he was establishing his encampment for the night and tending his goats. When we arrived, he was still in the process of unhooking the ten or so goats that had been pulling the wagon. About fifteen or twenty more goats wandered around, some eating grass and some drinking at the edge of the creek. He finished letting them all loose and tossed a few more chunks of wood on his growing fire.

We watched as he went over to the small, covered wagon and reached into the back. He lifted out two small goats that had been riding there. One was a baby goat, and the other was an older goat that looked like it had been born with no front legs. He carried the two of them down to the edge of the creek and held them down gently as he helped them take the drinks he knew they could not manage on their own.

After that, he put them back into the wagon and pulled out a couple of old coffee cans and a can of Austex Beef Stew. He pulled out a big knife and used it to cut the stew can open enough to dump the contents into one of the coffee cans, which he balanced on the edge of the fire to heat his dinner.

As we watched, he walked over to one of the female goats. He felt between her back legs to check her udder, decided that she had been nursing and didn't have any extra milk to spare, then moved on to more females until he chose the one he wanted. He straddled the goat's neck while he faced toward her rear, then reached down on each side of her milking while squirting milk into the empty coffee can until he had as much as he wanted. Then he spoke his first words out loud, "Anybody want to try a drink of goat's milk? Hit's good for what ails you! I drink it three times a day, and you can see how good I look!" Then he let out a long howling laugh and drank the goat's milk right out of the coffee can. Afterward, he stuck the never-washed can back in the wagon, pulled out a spoon, and proceeded to eat his beef stew from the other, now hot, coffee can.

Everyone there was staring intently at all of these doings. There was hardly a whisper. None of us had ever seen anything like this.

I was studying the little wagon all through this time. It was about half the size of what I thought a covered wagon would be and had steel wheels instead of wooden ones. A worn hand-painted sign sticking up from the top read, "Prepare to Meet Thy God!" A collection of tools, buckets, ropes, and other miscellany hung from the sides all the way around, and an assortment of license plates was nailed all around the edges. The Goat Man also seemed to have picked up the shreds of blown-out tires from along the road as he traveled and stuck them here and there wherever they could cling to the sides. Inside, I saw a bed where both he and the needy goats must have slept together.

After finishing his meal, he poked around in the wagon and came out with a handful of something. It turned out to be a variety of picture postcards of him, his wagon, and his goats taken at various places throughout their travels. "Here you are, folks," he started, "What you've been waiting for. Now you can prove to your friends and relatives that you have met and seen the real thing! Picture postcards for sale ... twenty-five cents each or three for a dollar!" Even though I knew that three for a dollar was more than twenty-five cents each, a lot of people laughed and handed him a dollar while he passed them only three postcards!

He finished selling the postcards and offered to let people have their picture made with him if they made "a free-will offering to the goats." Daddy was upset that we had been in such a hurry he had not thought to bring his Kodak. A few people had their pictures taken, but most didn't want to get that close to him or his smell.

Suddenly Daddy turned to Mama. "I'm going to go talk to him." Our Daddy was extremely extroverted and loved to talk with anyone! We were always the last people to leave the church when he finally had no one else to visit with. His desire to visit the Goat Man was no surprise to me.

"Joe," Mama frowned. "No ... he is nasty, and the smell! How can you stand it even from here? That fire stinks as much as he and the goats do. You've got your new suit on, and it will be ruined!"

He didn't argue. No, Daddy had left us standing where we were and was walking over to the fire, where we saw him stick out his hand and introduce himself to the Goat Man.

Mama was upset. All she wanted to do was get out of there and go home so we could eat our supper. She kept making faces at the stinking smell of the goats and the tire-burning fire. Daddy carefully kept his back to her so he couldn't see her giving him the evil eye.

While he was conversing with the Goat Man, Joe and I explored the goats and the wagon. The goats were a conglomeration of ages and sexes, and they all seemed to know and get along with one another. Some of the big Billy goats were tied to stakes driven into the ground, but the others just wandered around eating grass and weeds or lying on the ground, resting. They seemed to know that they were settled here for the night.

The more we looked at the wagon, the more stuff we saw. Anyone else would have called it junk, but I knew that we were surveying the Goat Man's treasures. A hay bale was tied crookedly to one side to feed the goats when no free grazing was available. Buckets hung from every spare hook and a wooden nail keg in which random lengths of water hose, several shovels, and a large garden rake kept company. More pieces of tires—ranging from whole tires to strips of rubber—and separated recaps were tied on any available hook. I didn't see a single space where anything else could have been tied or nailed on.

We saw that Daddy and the Goat Man were having a

great time together. They were talking and laughing like old friends. Mama just stood there glaring at both of them.

Finally, Daddy got up, shook hands with the Goat Man, and came over to gather us up to go home. "We better go on now because he is fixing to start preaching!" When we got back to the car, Mama got in the back seat with Joe and me. She said that Daddy smelled so bad that she would vomit if she had to ride in the front seat. Luckily, it was less than two miles back to our house.

"Don't even come in the house," she ordered Daddy. "I know that your new suit is ruined. You take it off on the back porch and do something with it. You can go right into the bathroom from there. We're not having supper until you take a good bath. You do something with that suit, so we can't smell it until you take it to the Dry Cleaners." He didn't argue. He had had his fun and was now happy to cooperate.

As soon as we sat down at the supper table, Joe and I were full of questions. We didn't have to ask them, though, because Daddy was ready to tell us the whole story.

"First of all," he started, "his name is not Goat Man. His real name is Ches McCartney, and he and I were born the same year, 1901."

Mama laughed out loud with this and commented, "Looked to me like he could have been born in 1801 from the condition he was in. Joe, that man has to be older than you!" We all laughed.

Daddy continued, "He said that his given name is 'Charles,' but he's been called Ches as long as he remembers. He has quite an interesting story." We were captured.

"Ches told me he was born on a farm out in a place called Keokuk County, Iowa. About 1915, when he was fourteen years old, he ran away to New York City. He hooked up with a Spanish woman who had a knife-throwing act. He would stand against a wooden wall with his legs apart, and his arms stretched out, and she—blindfolded—would throw knives that would stick in the wall all around him without hitting him. He said that she was ten years older than he was and that they actually got married! I don't know if I believed that, but that is what he said. After a while, though, she went off from him, and he went back home to the farm in Iowa and married a woman there whose name was Mable." At this, Mama turned away from the table. Her first name, which she hated, was "Mable," and I believe she thought Daddy was making this up just to annoy her.

Daddy went on. "When the depression came, the banks closed, and the farm went broke. He got a job working in forestry with the WPA. One day he was cutting down a big tree all by himself with nobody else helping him. When the tree fell, it fell on him and crushed his left arm and side. It knocked him out, and he was trapped under that tree for several hours. When the others came looking for him, they found him and thought he was dead. They took him to the undertaker. The undertaker was busy and didn't get around to him for a long time. Then, just when that undertaker started to stick the embalming fluid needle in his arm, Ches came to and sat up. Nearly scared the undertaker to death!

"Ches told me that God brought him back from the dead and that he became a Pentecostal Evangelical preacher after that. He didn't even go to the doctor after that accident, and his broken bones healed without any doctor's help. He showed me how crooked his left arm healed up so that he couldn't do manual labor after that."

Mama interrupted, "How did he get into this wandering goat business?" She was becoming interested by now.

"About this time, he read *Robinson Crusoe*, and the story gave him an idea. He got Mable to make the two of them, and the boy they had, outfits out of goatskins. He got the wagon from down at the train station where they lived in Iowa, put a top on it, got a bunch of goats, and they started wandering the country roads where he would preach to all the people they attracted.

"Mable got tired of this pretty soon. She took the boy and went back to Iowa. Ches, he just kept going! He figures that it was about 1942 when he started out. Says he's been to every state except Hawaii. After he told me all that, he said I would have to let him go since it was time for him to start preaching to all the people who had come to see him. He told me he had a little bit of land down in Georgia between Macon and Dublin, where he planned to start a church called the 'Free Thinking Christian Mission.' I figured that it was time for us to get out of there before the preaching started."

While we were eating our supper, my brother, Joe, and I asked Daddy all kinds of other questions. He told us a lot more stuff that the Goat Man told him about traveling with goats and living out in the open. It was all fascinating to us. I had a hard time going to sleep that night, trying to imagine what it would be like to live like that. I knew that I didn't want to do it, but it still was interesting to think about.

The next time we went down Eagle's Nest Road was on the way to church on Sunday. Daddy slowed down the car as we passed the Goat Man site. We looked at where the grass and weeds were either eaten off or mashed down and where the fire had burned down to nothing, but Mr. Ches McCartney was long gone.

Mama wanted to know what Daddy had done with his stinking new suit. He told her he had taken it out to the garage behind the house and that he would take it to the Cleaners in the coming week. He said that he was sure they could bring it back to life. We did not see or talk about the new suit after that. Everyone just acted like it had never existed.

Just when I was turning thirteen years old, we moved to our new house across town at a place called Hillside Terrace. It was after we moved there when the Goat Man came through again. One afternoon Daddy came home and told us, "The

Goat Man is back! I didn't hear where he spent the night last night. It wasn't the same place as the last time. But, he is on the move right now and is coming right past our house. I'm going to change my clothes right quick, and we can go and watch."

Mama thought this was funny since he had ruined his new suit the last time. He didn't even have on good clothes that day, but he was going to put something on that would not hurt to ruin. Mama, Joe, and I waited in the living room while Daddy went out into the laundry room where he kept his gardening clothes.

When he came back, we all burst out laughing. We smelled him before we saw him! He had taken his ruined suit after the first visit with the Goat Man and packed it away wrapped in a lot of plastic bags. He had brought it here when we moved, just waiting for this day. He had put his Goat Man suit back on so that he was ready for whatever happened on this day. It was hilarious. We all held our noses. "I wondered what ever happened to that suit," Mama smiled. "I figured that you took it to the Dry Cleaners and, when they told you it was hopeless, you had them throw it away and were then too embarrassed to tell us about it. I would never have guessed that you saved it, but, knowing you, I should have!" It was just the kind of thing our Daddy often did.

We now lived on the east side of Waynesville on the way toward Canton and Asheville. This was one of the only ways out of town. We walked down our driveway to the highway and just waited. There were no cars coming down the road from town. Daddy took this as a sign that the Goat Man and his goats had blocked all the cars and that he ought to be on the way soon. Sure enough, it was not long.

First, there was a Highway Patrol car coming very slowly down the road. "He must be warning the oncoming traffic to watch out. Nobody wants to come around a curve and find a road full of goats! I'll bet there's another one following in the back." Since ours was a pretty main road, a police escort seemed to me to be a good idea.

Then we saw them coming. The wagon and goat parade were the same as before, but this time we got to see them on the move. The overloaded wagon was being pulled by a dozen of the largest goats. The Goat Man was not riding but was walking alongside the pulling goats. Five or six large goats were tied to the back of the wagon, and all the others, including a good number of little ones, just followed along with the rest. Just as they got to our driveway, the road sloped up a bit. As the Goat Man felt the rise, he turned to the goats in the back and called out, "Need a little help ... need a little help!" and they put their heads against the back of the wagon and pushed it from there to help those pulling in the front. We were amazed.

There was a long line of cars following, and Daddy said, "Let's go get in the car and follow them. They can't be going far before they stop for the day." Daddy now had an old Pontiac that he drove to work. Mama agreed that we could follow them if we took that car so that he, in his Goat Man suit, would not stink up our good car.

We followed the parade down past Lake Junaluska, where he took the old road toward Clyde and Canton. This was a lot better because most of the following traffic could now go on the new road and not keep following. About halfway to Clyde, the Goat Man pulled off into a big field alongside the Pigeon River, where we parked so we could walk up and watch the Goat Man set up camp.

Since the Pigeon River at that time carried the pollution from the paper mill in Canton, we knew that even the goats could not drink out of it. But there was a little side stream that came through the field, and the loose goats headed straight for it. "I'll bet he's been here before," Daddy commented. "He knew exactly where he was going."

The routine was the same as last time. We helped gather sticks, and the Goat Man started the fire. He threw a big chunk of a recapped tire onto the fire. The goats all drank their fill before the larger ones were staked out. They all began to eat grass and weeds, but this time the Goat Man added some loose hay from the bale tied to the top of the wagon. He milked a goat, offered milk to anyone who wanted it, was turned down, and drank it all from the same old coffee can. He opened a can of something, heated, and ate his supper. Then Daddy made his move.

"I'm going to see if he remembers me." Mama didn't even

object; there was no point. We watched Daddy walk over and heard him call out "Ches McCartney ... nice to see you again!"

"Joe Davis! I was wondering yesterday if I was going to get to see you again." We watched them sit down and visit. I had a strange feeling at this moment. Could it be pride? My Daddy was neither afraid nor embarrassed to talk with anyone. Maybe I should learn something from him.

In fifteen or twenty minutes, they had finished their visit and said goodbye to one another. We headed back home before the preaching started. That was the last we ever saw of Mr. Ches McCartney, the famous Goat Man.

Before we even got out of the car back at home, Mama turned to Daddy and said, "You know what you're going to do with that suit this time, don't you?"

"You don't have to tell me," was all he said. Behind our house, we had what a lot of people had in those days: an old oil drum used for burning the trash. Daddy changed clothes in the laundry room, then he gathered up the trash that already needed to be burned and carried it, along with the stinking Goat Man suit, out to the incinerator. He got a good fire going, then took a stick and used it to hold the suit in the flames until it caught fire, then dropped it down into the barrel. By the time all the other trash had burned, there was no smell left of the Goat Man suit.

When I was working on the list of people whom I thought should be remembered in this collection of stories, it was pretty early when I thought of the Goat Man. But I also wondered what finally happened to him and his goats. Google helped me find the answer.

Ches McCartney continued to travel with his goats, claiming that they had covered more than a hundred thousand miles, until 1968. One night when he was camping in southeast Tennessee, he had been attacked and badly injured by someone who apparently thought there was something valuable in the old wagon. A number of his goats were also killed. After he woke up in the hospital with twenty-seven stitches in his head, he decided to give up the road.

With help from supporters, he was signed up for minimal Social Security benefits. He retired to his property in Georgia, where he had built a small wooden church. In later years, his house there burned. After living for a while in an old school bus, the Goat Man was moved into a nursing home in Macon, Georgia. He died there in 1998. Although he was 97 at the time, he claimed to be 106.

There will never be another Goat Man.

Chapter Five

Bill McInvaille

THE FIRST TIME I MET BILL McINVAILLE, we got in trouble.

I was in the third grade, and we had a new Sunday School teacher at the Methodist Church. Her name was Sarah Ann Judy. One Sunday, she told us that her daughter, Margaret, was going to have her fifth birthday party and that we were all invited since they were new, and Margaret didn't have many friends. On the following Saturday, my Mama took me to their address on Meadow Street, and there was the birthday party.

That is when I met Bill. He was Sarah Ann's half-brother, and he was the same age as I was. He lived with her, and so he was Margaret's uncle—at eight years old. Where they lived, Bill went to East Waynesville School. I did not know him, because I was in school at Hazelwood Elementary.

Refreshments were served, and presents were opened. Then everyone started playing with the new gifts. One of those presents was a Red Flyer wagon that Margaret just loved. To make everyone happy, Bill and I had the idea that, if she would get in the wagon, we would push her up and down the sidewalk. She had the tongue of the wagon pulled back into her hands so she could steer it while Bill and I pushed.

The first couple of times, we pushed her at a medium-slow pace since she was little. Then we got tired of that. We didn't talk about it; we just started pushing her faster. The old concrete sidewalk was bordered by maple trees, and the rhizome roots of the maple trees had pushed up sections of the sidewalk so that it was not all level or even. As Bill and I pushed her as fast as we could, and she screamed with delight, we hit one of the uneven sections of the sidewalk. The wagon tongue bounced out of her hands and over the front of the wagon. The tongue hit the sidewalk just in time to bring us to a dead stop when it hit the next uneven section of concrete. Six-year-old Margaret did not stop. She flew through the air and landed on the sidewalk face-first with a scream of terror followed by blood everywhere. Her mother came flying down the sidewalk, and her eyes could have burned bullseyes onto Bill's chest and mine.

My mother was called to come and get me. No matter how much I apologized, I knew that Sarah Ann was not going to be successful as my Sunday School teacher. Sure enough, they moved to the Presbyterian Church, and I did not meet Bill again until we ended up together in the seventh grade in Junior High School.

I am not quite sure how and why Bill and I became best friends in the seventh grade. We did not even have the same teacher. But soon, at lunchtime and after school, Bill, David Morgan, and I were constant companions.

David and I were in the band in the seventh grade, but Bill was not. He wanted very badly to be in the band, but his family could not afford an instrument. Bill did not give up. He kept on going to Mr. Campbell, our band director, repeating his pleas. By the beginning of the eighth grade, Mr. Campbell came up with an old, beat-up French Horn and told Bill that if he wanted to try it, he, as an eighth-grader, could be in the seventh-grade beginning band. Bill worked so hard that before the end of the first half of the school year, he had been moved up to the eighth-grade band. He never fell back but played that same beat-up French horn throughout high school.

By now, I deduced that Bill's home with Sarah Ann was very close to the bone financially. She was married off and on, two times married to and divorced from the same husband. They moved quite a lot from apartment to apartment and from house to house. The first time I went inside where Bill was living on Boundary Street, it was a tiny apartment carved out of a huge old house. The paint was faded, the wallpaper was peeling, and I knew that Bill's family would not be able to afford many things.

As soon as my mother met Bill, she was in love with him. He was a charmer, especially where women were concerned.

My Mama loved him and felt sorry for him at the same time. He was always welcome to ride home from school with us and more than welcome to spend time playing and eating at our house. He became another member of our family.

Every girl in high school loved Bill. He actually dated very little, but, somehow, he became the confessor that all the girls went to with their secret problems. They had what he called "seriousness talks" with him, and he held their information in complete confidence.

Bill was in all of our classes as well as in the band. In those days, this was called the "college preparatory" curriculum track. We all assumed we would go to college, and I never questioned whether Bill would be included in these plans.

He was the comic entertainer everywhere he went. Once in geometry class, he attempted to solve a problem by stating that "side by side equals side by side," an answer he repeated every time that he did not know the geometry answer. Every time Bill could not translate when he was called on in Latin class, he would seriously state that the translation was "Swiftly, swiftly, Caesar will carry water." This translation became the class standard whenever anyone did not know the answer.

When we went on band trips and went to eat in restaurants out of town, Bill would pretend that he was deaf and mute and would instantly begin made-up sign language with us. We instantly went along with him, even translating his order as he made cow-milking motions to indicate that he wanted a milkshake.

In our senior year, we all began to send off college applications. One day Bill announced that he was going to go to Florida State since another of his half-sisters lived there, and he could live with her to save money. Besides, if he moved down there, he would soon qualify for in-state tuition.

I applied and was accepted to Davidson College. When I told Bill that, he surprised me with what he said. "My dad went to Davidson. He graduated there back in the '30s. I don't remember him at all. I was too little when he died." I was too shy to ask him any more questions about that, but I was curious about how this new information affected the hard life Bill had lived so far.

The year we entered high school, the first public swimming pool was built in Waynesville. Mr. Lawrence Leatherwood, the school superintendent and our next-door neighbor, ran the pool in the summer. Bill applied for work there and kept that summer job every year, including the summer after we graduated. He was the darling of the swimming pool. In addition to working at the pool in the summer. Bill also worked with David and me as we ran the concession stand and the miniature golf course at the Waynesville Drive-In Theatre.

Summer came to an end following our graduations, and David, Bill, and I said goodbye to one another as we headed off in our separate directions. David went to King College in Bristol, Tennessee. He was going to go on from there to become a Presbyterian minister.

We all saw one another when we came home for Christmas. Bill didn't make it from Florida for Thanksgiving. We were sure that he couldn't afford the trip. The next summer, we were all back at the Drive-In at night while I worked at the Cokesbury Book Store at nearby Lake Junaluska during the daytime. Bill also continued his old job at the swimming pool.

The following year everything changed. Bill did not come home from Florida, and David didn't hear anything from him. We asked around to see if any of Bill's collection of girls had heard anything from him. Someone had heard that he had gotten a job in New York City at the World's Fair that was opening there. As it turned out, the Fair was so successful that it was held over, and instead of returning to school, Bill stayed in New York for what was to be more than an entire year.

We heard nothing from him during this time.

As a student at Davidson College, I sang in the Davidson Male Chorus. During spring break each year, the Male Chorus went on tour. These springtime tours were the first times in my life that I had ever traveled any distance at all from North Carolina. I loved the trips.

In my junior year, our trip headed north to Richmond, Washington, and on to New York. We were to sing on a Sunday afternoon at Fifth Avenue Presbyterian Church. The concert time arrived, and the chorus came out at the front of the sanctuary facing the audience. Immediately, I recognized the bushy black head of Bill McInvaille in the audience!

We were free for the evening following the concert, and Bill took me out on the town. We had a great time until about two in the morning when he accompanied me by subway back to the chorus hotel, where we said our goodbyes. That was the last time I saw him for thirty years.

By now, I was into my own young adult life and not as connected to home as when growing up there. Still, every time I was back in Waynesville, I would end up with someone who would ask, "Do you ever see Bill McInvaille or hear anything from him?" By now, his sister, Sarah Ann, had moved away from town, and so was not a source of information.

Whenever David and I were together, we would speculate and share whatever information we might have stumbled upon. One time David heard from someone traveling in Florida that they had seen Bill working as a waiter at a restaurant called The Kapok Tree around Tampa. Sometime later, there was another report that he was seen waiting tables at Burns Steak House in Tampa. Still, no one had any direct contact with him throughout this time. He had become a ghost.

In the early nineties, I was performing in Atlanta, telling stories. When the performance itself was over, and people were leaving the venue, I was gathering myself and getting ready to go. I looked up from packing merchandise and saw two women coming down the aisle toward the stage area. They looked vaguely familiar, but I could not place them. Then they got close, and it all came clear. It was Bill's half-sister Sarah

Ann and her now-grown-up daughter, Margaret. They had seen in the paper that I was to be there and had been at the performance.

We had a pleasant visit, but, all the while, I was afraid to ask about Bill. Nothing was offered. Finally, I could not hold back any longer, and I carefully asked, "Well ... tell me about Bill."

There was almost a scowl on her face as Sarah Ann answered, "He was drunk for twenty-five years. Then a judge who had seen him several times for DUI arrests gave him a choice between a 120-day commitment and 120 days in jail. Bill reluctantly chose the commitment.

"As soon as he went into rehab, he totally quit drinking. They said they had never seen anything like it. Just simply cold turkey. No more desire for alcohol.

"He went back to school and finished his degree and then got another one, I think, or maybe more. Now he is teaching down near Tampa." It was clear that she had told me more than she wanted to take the time to tell me, and the conversation was over. We said goodbye, and that was my total update on Bill.

As soon as I could contact David, I told him what I had learned. Sarah Anne had given me no indication that she had either an address or a telephone number to share. This made David and me wonder whether he was deliberately staying hidden from his past. Was he in some way embarrassed or ashamed about those lost years? We had no idea. Nor did we have any way to find out or search for him in a way that might not be rejected.

A half-dozen years passed with no new news about Bill. Whenever David and I were in touch, and sometimes even with other old friends, we would wonder. Is he dead or alive? Where might he be? What is the shape of his life like at this point? Is he in a meaningful or nourishing relationship with someone he loves and who loves him? We had nothing but questions.

It was Christmas, 1997. We were back in Waynesville. My mother was in nursing care at a place called Silver Bluff. In the year before, she had been diagnosed with cancer. In the follow-up to surgery, she had a stroke and lost her vision. Now she was cared for where we could visit her at will but not worry about her safety and comfort.

One of those days, when we were in Waynesville, we had just returned from a Silver Bluff visit when the kitchen telephone at my mother's house (my own teenage home) rang. No one had lived in the house for six months. I answered the phone expecting a solicitation call. Instead, it was, to my surprise, my best friend, David.

"Donald," he said, in his slow manner, "You're there."

"Yeah. We're up here visiting with Mama for these days before Christmas. What's up with you?"

"We are over at Aunt Kat's. Are you going to be there for

a little while?"

"Sure," I quickly answered. I had not seen him for a while.

"Don't go anywhere. I'll be over there in a few minutes."

I had no idea what was going on. I told my wife, Merle, that David was coming over in a few minutes, and we messed around looking forward to his visit.

I heard a loud-sounding vehicle coming up the driveway hill. It was David's old Volkswagen Van. Who knew how many miles were on this decade-old, beloved vehicle? Right behind it came another car, an unidentified Toyota.

There was a half-inch of snow on the ground as Merle and I walked out of the house to meet David and the Toyota's driver. "I brought somebody who wants to see you," David offered just as a person slid out of the Toyota. There he was, grinning the same silly grin from high school, thirty-five years and a few pounds later, Bill McInvaille!

In the next few minutes, those years fell away like magic. The three of us were laughing, talking, remembering, and telling stories like we had never been apart.

Bill did fill us in on a few things. After being prohibited from driving for ten years, he had finally gotten his license back. At about the same time, he inherited some money from an aunt he had long forgotten but who had not forgotten him. It had given him enough cash to buy "a car that would make it to North Carolina." He had come on this trip to visit my mother.

Way back in 1958, when the swimming pool was built, and Bill had applied for his job there, my mother had done something I never knew about. As I remembered, Mr. Lawrence Leatherwood, our School Superintendent, was the pool manager. He was also our neighbor and a dedicated friend of my parents. Mama had taught for him for years when he was still the principal of Hazelwood School before he became Superintendent.

She had secretly gone to him to tell him something. What she wanted to say to him was that he should hire Bill McInvaille and give him a summer job at the pool. "Those other kids who are applying don't need that job the way Bill does. They just want to get to spend the summer at the pool where their friends will be. Bill really needs the work and the money. He is a good boy, and I promise he will do a good job for you."

After Bill worked his five summers at the pool, Lawrence Leatherwood had told him that story. After all these years, it was now Bill's wish, since he could drive again, to come to Waynesville and thank my Mama for getting him that essential job.

David, Bill, and I spent the rest of the afternoon back at Silver Bluff with a visit that my mother enjoyed so much that she cried when it was over.

After that day, Bill was back in our lives. David and I had his address and phone numbers. More than that, every time I went to work in Florida, I would go to Tampa so he and I could head out to eat in Ybor City at the Columbia Restaurant. This was Bill's choice as it was one of the only places in Tampa where he had not worked during his active alcoholic years.

On one of those visits, he told me that working at a place like Burn's Steak House was a perfect place for an alcoholic. He didn't go to work until about five o'clock, and then there was booze all night and at closing. He could then sleep all morning until he was sober enough to start all over again. Every time he had been pulled over for driving drunk, he had been driving home from work after midnight. It was a perfect pattern.

In sobriety, Bill had returned to school. He graduated with a major in English. He went on to get his master's with a thesis on Caroline Miller, the mother of a high school friend of ours. Caroline Miller had won the Pulitzer Prize for literature in 1933 for her second novel, *Lamb in His Bosom*. Now Bill was back in school working on a Ph.D. about Thomas Hardy, a dark character indeed for a recovering alcoholic.

During the year before David, Bill, and I were to turn sixty, we were all at a high school band reunion when Bill got an idea. "Why don't the three of us all come to Ocracoke for a week in the summer and have a week-long sober birthday party?" The idea sounded great to David and me, so the planning commenced.

Christmas came that year. Sometime early in the season, Bill and I talked by phone. He was all excited about the planned birthday week. He even told me he was planning to fly to Norfolk and then rent a Mustang convertible to drive down for the week. We laughed and laughed. At the end of the call, Bill said, "You know that I love you."

I replied, "Yes, and you know that I love you, too." We said goodbye.

That year my wife, Merle, and I went to the John Campbell Folk School Winter Dance Week, where we arrived the day after Christmas. It was following the first evening's dance when we returned to our room, that I had a message on my new cell phone to call David's wife, Anne. I feared something had happened to David since he had a history of heart disease.

I called, and Anne answered. No, it was not about David. It was about Bill. His other half-sister Sandra had found David's number and had called it. On Christmas Eve, Bill had called 911 from his apartment. He had chest pain. The ambulance got him to the hospital, where they resuscitated him three times. The fourth try did not work. Bill was dead. (I was sure Anne had volunteered to call me; David was not up to it.)

We knew nothing about memorial plans. As it turned out, there were no plans. But a bit later, David and I decided that we would hold a memorial service at the Presbyterian Church in Waynesville, where we would announce the service in the *Waynesville Mountaineer* newspaper, and maybe some old friends would happen to come. Both of us were to speak.

When the day came, I arrived at the church to find the

parking lot nearly full of cars. So many friends from high school were there. Also, Sarah Ann's son, Parker, arrived. It was the right thing to do.

As summer neared, David thought we should go ahead and have the birthday party week. "We can talk about Bill," he laughed. "That will take more than a week." So we did. We even contacted Bill's half-sister, Sandra, and invited her to come to the island. We did not expect her to come from Florida, but we wanted her to know what we were doing.

David and his wife, Anne, arrived, and the following day another car pulled up at our house. It was Sandra and her current boyfriend. She had not come to stay for the week. "Just one night," Sandra insisted, but she had brought us something that she wanted to deliver in person. It was the canister holding Bill's ashes. "These ought to belong to you two boys. He loved you more than anyone. During his bad years, he was always afraid that you would find out how he was living and would be ashamed of him. I never saw him happier than when you finally got back together again. Now it's up to you to do whatever you think is right with the ashes." And she was gone the following day.

When Sandra departed, she left not only the ashes but also a thick envelope on the table. We opened it to find a ten-page letter from her telling her version of Bill's life. David and I sat down with the ashes between us and, for the first time, learned the unknown story of the early childhood of our best friend. We read and wept for most of that day.

Here is a brief capsule of what Sandra wrote to us:

Bill's mother was married to her first husband, the father of Bill's two half-sisters, when he died, leaving her a young widow with two pre-teenage daughters,

A few years later, she married again, and Bill was born. When he was only two years old, his father died of Bright's Disease. Bill's mother was widowed for the second time in six years.

When Bill was four, his mother began life in and out of alcohol rehabilitation, and Bill went to live with his two half-sisters, one of whom, Sarah Ann, was married by then.

The following year, his mother married again, this time to a prominent binge-drinking alcoholic attorney. This man doted on Bill, and this was the most stable time of his childhood.

Then, when Bill was nine, his mother was killed when two semi-trucks ran over the car she was driving.

We were told Bill's surviving step-father's family did not want him, so he was returned to live with Sarah Ann. That is when he came to Waynesville, and we first met at the birthday party.

There were many more details in the letter David and I read that day. Now we understood both how Bill ended up living such a struggling life by the time we knew him and how he had graces and manners beyond what we might have expected given his apparent economic state. We wept as we realized how, in our immaturity, we had failed to be the kind of friends we might have wished to be. We were also thankful that we had known and shared much of our growing-up lives with this beautiful person whose influence on those around him was exemplary in every way.

Now the ashes.

David and I thought a lot about what to do with them. We thought about taking them back to Waynesville, but we decided that it was only the two of us who were doing this and we should put them in a secret place only we would know about and could visit on occasion. We decided to spread them somewhere on Portsmouth Island, next door to Ocracoke, where Merle and I lived.

In the 1700s, Portsmouth Village was the largest town on the coast of North Carolina. In those days, Ocracoke Inlet was the only way to get from the Atlantic Ocean to the Pamlico Sound and then to the mainland. The problem was that with the average sound depth of just over twenty feet, the deep draft oceangoing sailing ships could not safely cross to the mainland. Portsmouth was the place where the giant sailing ships unloaded their wares into warehouses, from which they were transferred to "lighters," shallow-draft boats that took things to the mainland.

With the advent of steam power, Portsmouth began to die. The last residents left in 1971, and today Portsmouth is a charming ghost town within the Cape Lookout National Park.

The only way to get there is by private boat.

David and I planned the day to come. We were taking a picnic, along with the ashes. We would explore all around the island and then decide where we would leave our "treasure" of Bill's ashes.

The day we went over, no one else was on the island. We had the whole place to ourselves. It was very windy, and the wind kept away the insects that sometimes haunt visitors there. After visiting the old store and Post Office, the old Methodist Church, and several old houses around the village, we ended up at the former Life Saving Station for our picnic lunch. We ate on the porch, then climbed the steps to the lookout tower on the top of the building.

As we looked down from above, David suddenly pointed and asked, "Are those oysters down there?" Sure enough, we were looking down into oyster beds in the water of the Sound. "Bill was the first person I knew who actually ate an oyster! Let's go put some of the ashes down there. He would like that, and we will remember it." I agreed.

We climbed down from the tower, retrieved the ashes from the backpack, and headed out to the edge of the water by the oyster bed. The wind was blowing hard. David opened the container and shook some ashes into his hand. He said a few words to bless us with Bill and tossed the ashes into the water. Now it was my turn.

I took the now-open canister in my left hand and turned

it to shake more ashes into my right hand. Just as the ashes were beginning to leave the canister, the wind caught my hat to blow it off. There was no thought process; it was pure reflex. My left hand, holding the open canister, reached for the departing hat. The result was that I threw all of Bill's remaining ashes directly into my own face.

Ashes were all over me. They were in my sweaty hair, in my eyes, up my nose, in my mouth, and down the open neck of my shirt. I was wearing Bill! At the same time, I saw that David was rolling on the ground laughing his head off. "He's here! He's here! Bill is here! No one else could have thought that up but Bill!" I laughed in agreement.

We shook as much onto the ground as we could, but as we rode the boat back home to Ocracoke, I could feel gritty Bill all over me.

Once back home, two things were done. First of all, I knew that I would never wear that particular hat again. No, it was (and is) preserved. Its rim contains a good bit of what was left of Bill. Secondly, I decided to shower outdoors rather than inside the house. No matter how troublesome he was in life, I did not think that some of Bill's remains should end up in the septic tank. Instead, with the outdoor shower, they ended up nourishing the rosemary bushes that surround it.

Now, each time we travel to Portsmouth, my heart contains a story much too large to tell in one day.

Chapter Six

The Plott Hound

IF YOU DROVE UP PLOTT CREEK ROAD outside of Waynesville, North Carolina, in 1950, our house was the first house on the right-hand side of the road. It was maybe a quarter of a mile up the then-unpaved road from where you left the pavement of Sulfur Springs Road behind.

Plott Creek itself ran down the back side of our property, which included a huge garden plot, our small white bungalow house, our cow pasture, and a chicken yard.

Directly across the road from our house was a large hay field, beyond which stood the George Plott house. Up the road a little way was the John Plott house. Nearby were the Vaughn Plott house and the Mont Plott house. There was no question as to why this was Plott Creek Road.

Today the Plotts are more famous than they were then, all because of a dog. Around 1750, Johannes Georg Plott, age sixteen, left the Bavarian part of Germany to come to America with his brother. They brought with them five dogs described as Hanover Schweisshunds, three striped and two yellow.

Johannes' brother died on shipboard and is long forgotten, but Johannes and his dogs settled in what became North Carolina. His son, Henry, began to breed the original dogs and their descendants with carefully chosen local dogs. He created "Plott's hound," a dog particularly bred for bear and later boar hunting.

In 1989 the Plott Hound became the official State Dog of North Carolina. Since 2006, it has been recognized by the American Kennel Club and competes in the Scent Hound Division.

These dogs are wonderfully loyal, alert, and intelligent. Weighing in at about sixty-five pounds, they range in color from black to blonde, with most being a lovely brindle blend of those two colors. Their long legs enable them to run rapidly through the undergrowth. They will chase their prey until they can no longer run and often have to rest up for a day before returning home.

There were Plott hounds throughout the neighborhood when I was a child.

In those days, most dogs ran free, and the hounds were no exception. It was common for us to have Plott hounds from up and down Plott Creek visiting our house at any time. We knew most of them, or at least my Daddy knew them. He would say, "That's John Plott's dog," or "That's one of Mont's dogs." My mother was terrified of the big dogs even though they were as gentle to a child as they could possibly be. (She must have had some kind of childhood trauma with dogs, as she was always afraid of any sort of dog.)

My mother did not know that I had a secret Plott hound! Beside our house was a huge garden. The garden was as large as the entire lot on which our house stood, including our front and back yards. It was, on the side, separated from the yard of our house by a privet hedge that was about five feet tall. It was then, on the front, separated from Plott Creek Road by a tall row of hemlock trees. I loved to play in the garden, behind the hedge, and under the hemlock trees.

One day we came home from somewhere. I have no idea where we had been or what day of the week it might have been. It does not matter. Mama went into the house, and, since it was a pleasant day, I stayed outside to play by myself. Pretty soon, I found myself behind the privet hedge playing in the garden.

I wandered over toward the hemlock trees. You could hide under the hemlock trees and spy on all the cars that went up Plott Creek Road. I thought this was a big deal in that I could see the people in the cars doing things they did not know I was seeing.

Just as I got to the trees, I spotted the dog.

The ground under the hemlock trees was thickly carpeted with dry, brown hemlock needles. It made a soft floor under those big trees. Right there, curled up and asleep in a bed she had wiggled out of the hemlock needles, was a big, brindled Plott hound. She was breathing deeply and, once in a while, would let out a sigh in her sleep. She was a beautiful dog, and I instantly loved her. Since my mother would never let me have a dog of any kind, I secretly adopted this beautiful dog as my own.

The dog had a collar with John Plott's name on it. That made no difference to me. All this meant was that I did not have to feed and take daily care of my dog. She would be mine when she came down here to nap under our hemlock trees and his when she went home for supper. About three days each week, my dog was under the hemlock trees enjoying what I decided was her vacation home. She could sleep there, where I could pet her and talk to her. That is all either of us needed from one another. I never told my mother anything at all about the dog.

Every Sunday, our family went to the Methodist Church in Waynesville. We almost never missed a Sunday. Our Sunday School teacher during this time of my life was Coach Weatherby. Coach Weatherby was both the principal and the head football coach at Waynesville Junior-Senior High School. I think they got him to teach the upper elementary Sunday School class so he would have all of us broken in before we got to the seventh grade.

We loved having Coach Weatherby as our Sunday School teacher. He had so many school stories and football stories that he had stories to go with every verse in the Bible! Mr. Weatherby didn't have to prepare his Sunday School lesson because he had so many stories from his forty years of coaching and being principal. We would just get to Sunday School, and one of us would be asked to read the Bible lesson for the day. Then, Coach would start in and tell us stories to go with the Bible story. We did enjoy Sunday School with him.

Our arch-rivals in sports at Waynesville High School were the Canton Black Bears. Football was the ruling sport. Every year Waynesville and Canton played not one but two football games. There was the official conference game played as scheduled by the Smoky Mountain Conference during the regular season. Then there was the second and unofficial game. This game was played the afternoon of Thanksgiving Day and was called the "Paper Bowl" after Champion Paper and Fibre Company, the largest employer in the county.

Everyone who had grown up in Waynesville came home for Thanksgiving and looked forward to the big game. The total county population was fewer than ten thousand people, and it was estimated that more than twelve thousand fans were often in attendance at the Paper Bowl. Every law enforcement person in Western North Carolina was on duty for the game, and a temporary woven-wire fence was erected between the stands and the field to keep fights down and people off the field. It was quite a day for everyone.

On the year in question, the regular season game had, to incredible frustration, ended in a tie. This made the Paper Bowl game more important than ever. A record crowd was on hand. The game progressed relatively evenly without much passing and with hard ground play by both teams. Near the end of the fourth quarter, we got the ball with just over a minute on the clock. Canton was leading on the scoreboard by thirteen to twelve. The ball moved down the field on the next three plays. Following a time-out, six seconds remained on the clock. Our team had the ball inside the twenty-yard line. The plan was obvious: we only needed two points to avoid a loss, and we were in a perfect position for a field goal. Both teams lined up, knowing what was in the air.

During the time-out, no one had noticed that one Canton back fielder had taken off his cleated shoes and tossed them off the end of the field. He lined up barefooted about two steps behind their center lineman as everyone waited for the ball to be snapped.

Just as the ball was snapped and being put on the tee for our kicker, the Canton back fielder ran, in his bare feet, up the back of his own center lineman. As he did, that giant lineman stood up, and the back fielder launched from his shoulders high in the air, blocked the field goal kick, and landed right on top of our kicker. Without time to think but with the instinct of pure revengeful rage, our kicker drew back and slugged that

Canton player in the side of the face giving him both a broken nose and the onset of a monster black eye. The two of them were in an instant slugfest. Teeth flew, knocked out in addition to the broken noses and black eyes that marked both teams. Whistles blew, and red penalty flags flew all over the field just as the horn blew, announcing the game's end.

The officials finally decided that there were so many penalties that they must surely cancel each other out. The final score stood cruelly at thirteen to twelve. It was a horrible afternoon to be called Thanksgiving!

Three days later, Sunday came. Our family got up that morning, had Sunday pancakes, and got ready to go to Sunday School and church. We were all still sore over the ball game. We got to Sunday School, and, totally out of character, Coach Weatherby arrived slightly late for the class to start. He did not look good.

We all just sat there while Mr. Weatherby slowly picked up the Sunday School book and turned to the page for this day's lesson. "Well," he started, "We have been studying the Sermon on the Mount for several weeks now. I guess that today's lesson is still on those chapters. Here, Chuck," he handed the Bible to one of my friends, "Why don't you read today's lesson for us. It is from Matthew five, verse thirty-eight through verse forty-five."

Chuck took the Bible and flipped through the pages until he found Matthew. Then he went a page at a time until he got to chapter five. We could all see his finger going down the page until he stopped to read at verse thirty-eight. He cleared his throat and began.

"You have heard that it was said, 'An eye for an eye and a tooth for a tooth.' But I say to you, do not resist one who is evil. But if anyone strikes you on the right cheek, turn to him the other also; and if anyone would sue you and take your coat, let him have your cloak as well; and if anyone forces you to go one mile, go with him two miles. Give to him who begs from you, and do not refuse him who would borrow from you. You have heard that it was said, 'You shall love your neighbor and hate your enemy.' But I say to you, Love your enemies and pray for those who persecute you, so that you may be sons of your Father who is in heaven; for he makes his sun rise on the evil and on the good, and sends rain on the just and on the unjust." Then Chuck handed the Bible back to Mr. Weatherby, and he sat down.

Mr. Weatherby took the Bible and just stood there for a long time. Finally, he cleared his throat and looked solemnly at us. "Boys and girls," he started, "That was a long time ago." Then he started telling us unrelated football stories.

After church, we got in the car and headed home. Just as Daddy drove up Plott Creek Road and started to turn in our driveway, there at the edge of our yard stood Robert Hester. We all knew Robert. He was not married and lived up the road from us. Robert was, my Mama said, the funniest-looking person she had ever seen. He had no teeth, a long, straight nose, and a long, skinny chin. Mama said she thought you could lay a ruler from the crown of his head to the tip of his chin, and you couldn't see light under it. (I tried and tried to figure out what that would look like, and I couldn't visualize it, but it sounded funny to me, too!)

Robert had a long history with our family. He was that community fellow who could be hired to do any kind of dirty work that you didn't want to do yourself. At various times, Daddy had hired Robert to burn bagworms out of the apple trees, to get sparrow nests out of the gables of the house, and to dig the willow roots out of the septic tank lines. I could only remember one time when Daddy tried to hire Robert to do something that Robert would not do. Daddy once asked Robert if he would dig the poison ivy off the bank between the garden and the creek.

Robert almost ran off when he heard the request. He just kept backing up from Daddy and saying, "No... No... No! I can't do that. That stuff just about chases me, and if it gets on me, I puff up and swell up all over. It makes my eyes swell shut. I keep medicine from the doctor at home all the time just for an emergency. No ... I can't do that!"

Robert had one great talent. He could somehow always manage to show up at your house just when it was time to eat! This was especially true when Sunday or holiday dinners were about to go on the table.

(One time, Robert showed up at our house in the fall of the year, and Mama invited him to come in and have something to eat with us. It was the middle of the day. We sat down at the table, and Daddy asked a blessing. We all started eating. After about twenty minutes, Robert turned to Daddy and asked, "Mr. Joe, why are you burning your barn?

Daddy had been burning leaves out near the barn. When Mama called him to come in and eat, he raked the burning leaves apart and thought they would just burn themselves out. Instead, the wind had blown the blazing remnants into the barn, and the old wooden barn was on fire. Robert had seen the fire, but he accepted Mama's dinner invitation and ate for twenty minutes before he said anything about it. (We knew all about his priorities!)

So, on that Sunday, as we turned in the driveway and saw Robert lingering there, Mama rolled down her window and spoke to him. "Hello, Robert. We are just about to have Sunday dinner. Why don't you come inside and eat with us?"

"I'd be much obliged," Robert replied, and as Daddy drove on down our driveway, Robert followed the car and came around to the back door with all of us. We got out of the car and started up the steps to the back porch when Robert caught up with us. He looked up at Mama and said, "Mrs. Davis, there's a big old Plott Hound out there in your front yard. Do you want me to get rid of it?" He knew that Mama was scared of all kinds of dogs.

Robert didn't wait for Mama to give him an answer. He just seemed to assume that her answer was yes. He walked back up the driveway toward the front yard and said over his shoulder, "I'll be right back."

"What's he going to do?" I asked Daddy as we walked into the kitchen from the porch.

"Oh, I reckon he's just going to chase some wandering dog out of our yard." Suddenly, from where we were in the back of the house, we all heard the most terrible sound that to this day I have heard in my life. It was the high-pitched scream of a dog being thrashed.

Daddy took off running through the house to the front door, and I followed right behind him. Just as he opened the door, we saw *my* Plott Hound cowering around the privet hedge that separated the yard from the garden. Then I saw Robert drop on the ground the tree limb with which he had been whipping the dog.

"That was unnecessary, Robert," Daddy called out in a loud voice as Robert came back toward the house. The tone of Daddy's voice was trembling with anger, and I knew that more words were to come later, but not on this side of Mama's Sunday dinner.

There was a palpable chill in the room as we gathered at the table, and Daddy seemed to tremble through the blessing. There was no conversation as we passed the food and began to eat. Robert kept his head down as he gummed his food, seeming to feel that he had done something beyond approval.

As Robert ate, we began to notice something. His face began to turn red, and his eyes were watering and swelling. At the same time, his fingers were blushing and starting to puff up until they looked like tight sausages. We all began to guess what was happening.

In our front yard, there were two huge red maple trees. One of the trees had a thick, hairy-looking poison ivy vine growing up into it. Mama had begged Daddy, again and again, to cut the poison ivy out of the tree, but he said he "wanted to see just how big it would get." When Robert had reached, without looking, up into the maple tree to grab a limb to thrash the dog, he had mistakenly gotten hold of a woody autumn poison ivy branch instead. He had whipped the Plott Hound with the poison ivy limb, wiped the sweat off his face with the back of his hands, and discarded the ripe limb on the ground before coming inside to eat.

As we realized what had happened, Robert himself came to the same realization. "I better go on home," he told us.

"Do you want me to take you to the hospital or to find a doctor?" Daddy offered.

"No, I'll just go home and start in on my medicine," he almost whispered. "Thank you for the dinner, Mrs. Davis. I am much obliged." He then picked up his hat and walked through the house and out our front door.

When we heard Robert stumble on the porch, we realized that his eyes were so swollen he could not see where he was going. By the time Daddy and I followed to see, Robert had stopped and was sitting on the top step of our front porch. His elbows were on his knees, and his face was in his hands. He seemed to ponder what he should do next. Just as Daddy was about to insist that he take him to the hospital, he and I saw something.

The Plott Hound, my secret Plott Hound, was creeping back out from behind the privet hedge. She was almost slinking very close to the ground as she came around the edge of the yard and toward the front porch of our house. "Let's just watch and see what happens," Daddy quietly ordered me.

"I think she's going to get Robert," I told Daddy.

"Wait and see," was all he said.

The dog kept coming, sneaking silently under the edges of the low juniper bushes that fronted the porch. Now the hound was only about ten feet from Robert, who neither saw nor heard the dog.

The Plott Hound kept coming, and Robert had no idea that the dog was upon him until he felt the warm moisture of the dog licking his hands!

The sweet dog licked Robert's hands and then his face. She licked him over and over, and Robert just sat there, seeming to be comforted by the wetness and the care.

Then the dog nudged Robert until he stood up. The Plott

Hound got hold of Robert's shirt cuff and began to lead him across our yard and up the road. My Plott Hound knew where Robert lived.

All was silent until Daddy almost whispered to me, "Son, that dog is a better man than Robert Hester.

I quietly answered back, "Yes, Daddy, and that dog is a better Sunday School teacher than Mr. Weatherby."

Chapter Seven

Mr. Campbell

IT WAS THE FIRST DAY OF SCHOOL in the seventh grade. I was in Mrs. Margaret Pilarski's room at Waynesville Junior High School. On the morning of that first day, Mrs. Pilarski asked us a question that we, as students, had never been asked before. "Students," she began, "It is time for us to make some choices about our extracurricular activities." (In six years of school, we students had never been asked to make choices!)

"How many of you boys," she went on, "Think that you would like to play football?" I did not move. I do not remember how much I weighed in the seventh grade, but it is documented that I weighed eighty-nine pounds when I got my driver's license at age sixteen. I kept my hands very low to be sure there could be no misinterpretation. Many of the bigger boys raised their hands.

"Now," she continued, "How many of you girls think you might like to be cheerleaders?" Several girls' hands went up, and Mrs. Pilarski wrote their names down.

Then she asked, "How many of you think you would like to be in the band?" I didn't even think about this; I just watched my hand as it seemed to rise voluntarily while I thought, "I guess I am going to be in the band!"

The following night, my parents took me to the Band Building between the Junior High and the High School so I could buy an instrument. I had decided on the trumpet, and on that very night, my Daddy shelled out sixty dollars to buy me a beautifully used and barely dented King trumpet. I was a member of the band.

It was also that night when I first met David Morgan, who was to be my best friend throughout High School and for the coming sixty years.

I had not met David before as we lived on opposite sides of town and had gone to different elementary schools. He lived with his grandmother, his Aunt Ruth, Uncle Phil, and his Aunt Dot. David's mother died when he was an infant, and he was raised by her whole family after that. He had been brought to pick an instrument by Aunt Ruth, who happened to work with my Daddy at the bank. As soon as they saw each other, David and I were introduced, and we were instantly best friends.

David had decided he wanted to play the alto sax, and for the same amount Daddy had spent on me, Aunt Ruth shelled out sixty dollars and bought David a Selmer alto sax. He always said he got a better deal than I did because his saxophone came with a whole box of used reeds!

That night we also met our seventh-grade band teacher, Mr. Bob Campbell.

Mr. Campbell was quite a character in Waynesville. He had graduated from Davidson College a half-dozen years before and had turned down going into business with his father to become a band director. He had been given a new Plymouth as a college graduation present by that same father. The Plymouth lived in its garage in all but the most wretched weather. Meanwhile, he insisted on riding a small motor scooter everywhere he went. He could be seen riding all over town. In the winter, his ear-muffs and overcoat caught the breeze.

We all loved Mr. Campbell right from the first day of class. We had been warned by the eighth graders that he was very strict and no-nonsense, but we discovered his fairness from day one. We actually loved his strictness as it communicated to us his belief that we were capable of accomplishing things that a person with fewer expectations might never have communicated. It was an honor to have him believe in us so strongly. We worked as hard as we could to rise to his expectations and not disappoint him.

I shall always remember the first time we had what we learned to call "tryouts." We had been learning a little march by F. E. Bigelow entitled "Our Director." We thought we had gotten pretty good at it when he announced the tryouts day.

On that day, we each had to get up and play our own part, along with a record of the march, while we marched in a rectangle, sixteen steps on each side and eight steps on each end, right on the floor in front with the whole band watching us.

My turn came, and I played my melody part on the trumpet as well as I could, considering my nerves. I believe that I made over a hundred shaky mistakes (and the march only had sixty-four bars!).

When it was all over, Mr. Campbell began to announce the results. In each section of the band, the top person in each instrument was named "first chair," and lesser achievers fell in below as second, third, fourth, and so on. I could not believe my ears when in the trumpet section, I was named "first chair."

But ... the announcement was followed by a qualifier. Mr. Campbell said, "Yes, I have decided that Donald is to be first chair, but I need to tell you why. You see, in the mistake department, he was not tops. In fact, in the mistake department, he was way on up there. But, he did something that no one else in the whole band did, and it needs to be an example and a lesson for all of us. Whenever he made a mistake, he did not try to back up and fix it. He just kept right on going and never broke the rhythm of the music. If you are going to play together as a band, you cannot back up and fix mistakes. You have to learn just to keep going!"

It was years later when I realized that this lesson was not just about being in the band. It was about all of life.

We worked very hard through the fall of the year with the promise from Mr. Campbell that, if we did well, we might get to play one number at the beginning of the Christmas Concert before the High School Band played their entire planned program. We did work hard, and in November, he told us we were almost ready to play the Jingle Bells Medley before the Eighth Grade Band also played at the concert beginning. But, to be really prepared, we needed to add an extra Tuesday night practice for the final four weeks prior to the concert date.

He explained it to us: "We will practice each Tuesday night for exactly one hour beginning this Tuesday at seven o'clock. Don't be late."

Tuesday arrived, and that day my friend, David, went home with me so my Mama could take us both to the practice and then deliver David home for the night. He ate supper with us, and then at about twenty minutes until seven, we got in the car, and Mama drove us to the band building. We were there ten minutes early, which also seemed true of the other band members.

At precisely seven o'clock, by the big clock on the wall, Mr. Campbell came out of his office, picked up his baton, and we began to practice the Jingle Bells Medley. We played until eight o'clock, and we just kept on playing. At five past eight, we were still playing. We were looking at our music and at the big clock at the same time, remembering that he had said "precisely one hour" and he was not a person to be untruthful.

At twelve and a half minutes past eight, he suddenly put his baton down right in the middle of a phrase of music and announced, "That's exactly one hour ... you can all go home now."

"Wait," a whole chorus of voices confronted him, "We started at seven o'clock ... that was more than an hour."

He smiled at us, "It is true," he started, "that some of you were here ready to begin at seven o'clock. But, several were late, and the last person to arrive, Mister Rabbit McCracken, did not get here until twelve and a half minutes past seven. You need to understand that if we are going to be a band, we are not actually in rehearsal until everyone is here. Until we are all here, we are just warming up!"

It was also a long time when I realized that this, too, was not just about being in the band—it was also about all of life.

All through that seventh-grade year, being in the band was the high point of my school life. The band was where I met almost all my friends who would last through high school and beyond. Mr. Campbell was the person we all worked hardest to please because he believed in us and expected so much from us. By springtime, we joined with the eighth-grade band to play two numbers before the High School Band's Spring Concert.

When we got to the end of that seventh-grade year, Mr.

Campbell told us that being in the eighth-grade band was going to be much more serious. We were going to have an extra week-night practice every Tuesday night throughout the eighth grade, and we were going to have summertime rehearsals once a week for the four weeks of August before school started in September. All summer, we looked forward to that. It was like a special promotion we all felt we had achieved.

We all received letters from Mr. Campbell telling us that the eighth-grade band would have August pre-school rehearsals at ten o'clock each Tuesday morning of that month. When the first Tuesday of August came, my Mama took me and picked up David on the way so we would get to the band building by at least 9:45! Everyone was appropriately early, and at about five to ten, Mr. Campbell declared that we were on time, passed out our new music, and the rehearsal began. It was obvious from the start that most of us had kept practicing through June and July, as we sounded as good as we had when school ended in late May.

We were most of the way through the hour when the door to the practice room opened and Mr. Bowles, the Waynesville School Superintendent walked in unannounced. He did not even wait for the number we were playing to come to an end before interrupting Mr. Campbell and pulling him aside for a serious conversation. We could all see and feel the tension in the air as their conversation went on. No one could actually hear what was being said, but we could see Mr. Bowles doing most of the talking and Mr. Campbell shaking his head and handing back to Mr. Bowles a bunch of papers that had been pushed into his hands.

Suddenly, Mr. Bowles turned on his heels and marched out of the band room letting the door slam behind him. The atmosphere was cold. Mr. Campbell was shaking as he turned to face us. He started, "Boys and girls, this is the end of our before-school practice plan. You may all be free to use the office telephone if you need to call parents to pick you up early. I will be here if you want to wait until they had planned to come for you anyway. He then walked into a small piano practice room and closed the door behind him.

It was only about fifteen minutes until Mama was to pick us up anyway, so David and I just waited around for her to arrive; we knew she would be early. On the ride home, we told her what had happened, and she got me to tell the whole story to Daddy again that night at the supper table. He just shook his head and said, "I don't think this can be good."

Since it was still summertime and school was still out, we did not know anything until Daddy came home from work the next afternoon and told us: "Bob Campbell is gone. He packed up and left town, they said, before the day was over yesterday afternoon ... didn't even spend another night in town after that meeting with Buck Bowles." For the next thirty-three years, that was the end of the Mr. Campbell story, as far as anyone knew.

When school started in September, we had a new band director, Mr. Dale Ratcliffe. Nothing was ever said at school about Mr. Campbell's departure. My Daddy's only comment about our new teacher was, "I'll bet that Charlie Isley (the High School band director) will leave pretty soon since he doesn't have Bob Campbell to prepare perfect students for him by the time they get to high school. (And he did!)

As time went on, we heard that Mr. Campbell was living and teaching in Glendale, California. One time it was reported that someone thought they had seen him in the audience at the end of the *Lawrence Welk Show* when audience members got up and danced. That was all that we heard.

In 1991 I had a performance at a place called The Stompin' Ground in Maggie Valley, not five miles from Waynesville. The audience was filled with childhood friends and relatives as well as others. When the storytelling performance had finished, I was talking with Ernestine Upchurch, a dear friend for many years. As we talked, Ernestine asked me: "Are you on the road? Where are you going from here?" I told her that my wife, Merle, and I were on our way to California where I had performances in Monterey and then in Bakersfield.

"Bakersfield?" she was startled, "Do you remember Bob Campbell who used to be the Junior High and Assistant Band Director here?"

"Of course I do," I answered. "I was in the last class that

he started out when I was in the seventh grade. He left after that."

"I was in high school," Ernestine went on. "He and I had kept up with Christmas cards and an occasional note since then. He is retired and lives in Bakersfield. You ought to try to find him." In my mind, a plan was hatched.

That year my wife, Merle, and I drove out to the west coast. We had several jobs both in California and along the way. Since we were in Monterey the week before going to Bakersfield, I decided that it was time to make the call and see if I could locate Mr. Campbell. It was in the years before cell phones were universal and everyone still had a landline; it was also possible to dial information and find someone's phone number.

I called 411 and asked for Bakersfield information. "Do you have a number for a Mr. Robert A. Campbell?" I even remembered his middle initial.

In a moment the operator came back on the line. "Yes, we have a number that is listed for an R. A. Campbell. Could that be it?" I wrote down the number and waited about an hour before making the call. Just getting the number was an emotional rush for me. Finally, I dialed the number.

"Hello," a cheerful voice answered. "This is Bob Campbell. May I help you?" Even after more than thirty years, the voice was recognizable, and I could envision him on the other end of the line.

I started, "Were you once a band teacher in Waynesville, North Carolina?"

"Who is this? Is this Ernie Edwards?" Ernie Edwards was a band member who was a year older than I and surely one of those students whom a teacher would never ever forget!

"No," I went on, "This is Donald Davis." There followed that kind of silence that it is impossible to fix. It was the kind of dead pause that loudly proclaims, "I have no idea who you are."

I tried to redeem the moment, "I was in the seventh-grade band the last year you were in Waynesville ... I played trumpet."

He perked up and very dearly tried to pretend that he remembered me, but it was too late. I knew that he did not. "How are you doing, Donald? Where are you and what are you doing now?"

I explained that I was a storyteller and that I was coming the following week to do a performance at the Beale Library. I was wondering if we might get together while I was there.

"Beale Library? Why that's my library! I volunteer there several times a week and I'm in and out of there almost every day! That's great. Why don't I make the plans and we can have an early dinner and then we can go to the program together. I would like that ... I can introduce you to some people." Now there was no retreat; I was set to meet with the lost Mr. Campbell after three decades.

The next week came. We drove from Monterey to

Bakersfield and checked in to the hotel where the library was keeping us. After learning where we were staying, I called Mr. Campbell back and left a message telling him where we would be on that day and leaving him the number. I had heard nothing since then.

When we arrived in Bakersfield, we had been traveling for several days without the benefit of a laundry. While I settled in the room, Merle headed out in the car to take our dirty clothes to a drop-off laundry where they would be ready for us the next morning. While she was gone, the telephone in the room rang. It was Mr. Campbell. He was down in the lobby of the hotel— early of course—waiting to take us to dinner.

"My wife took our laundry out to get it done and she is not back yet," I tried to explain.

He responded, "Well, she better get back. I have gotten my favorite Basque restaurant to let us in early so we would have plenty of time to eat and visit before you need to be at the library. Come on down here and we can talk until she gets back. I hope it's not long!"

I had another idea: "Sometimes she can be late. Why don't we leave her directions about where we are going, and I can go ahead and ride with you to the restaurant?"

"You can't ride with me!" he laughed. "I'm on my motorbike!" Now I knew for sure that I had the right person.

Fortunately, Merle returned very soon, and we got in our car to follow him. Follow him we did, me driving and trying to keep up with a seventy-year-old man changing lanes in one-hundred-and-five-degree heat on a freeway in Bakersfield!

Once at the restaurant, we followed his advice on the Basque menu selections and ordered our meals.

"I have a confession to make," Mr. Campbell started. "When you first called, I had no idea who you were. I am afraid that I did not remember you. I tried to act like I did, but, honestly, I didn't. After we hung up, I called Ernestine back in Haywood County so she could fill me in. As soon as she told me who your parents were, I put it all together.

"Your daddy was Mr. Joe at the bank. He was a wonderful person and a great help to me as a young teacher getting started. He helped me set up my first bank accounts when I got to Waynesville in 1953 and was always ready to be supportive of and helpful to any band projects we had.

"One summer I had an opportunity to go to Europe on a music tour. I wanted to go so badly, but I didn't have any money to make a trip like that. Charlie Isley must have told your daddy about the trip because one day Mr. Joe called me on the phone and told me he wanted to see me at the bank. I was afraid that I had overdrawn my account or made some kind of mistake.

"When I got there, Mr. Joe told me that he had heard about the European trip and that I should go. I told him I didn't have any money to make the trip. He then told me that I might not have another opportunity like that and that he would have the bank loan me the money on my signature alone so I could make the trip and pay the loan back a little bit at a time. It was a wonderful summer, and I managed to pay the loan off in two years!"

We ate and visited and had a wonderful time as we filled in the lost years since 1958. He had been a band director in Glendale for many years and then in Bakersfield until he retired. At the end of his career, he had actually also taught the beginnings of computer science as well as music.

All of a sudden, a new topic came up. "Say," he began with, a serious expression on his face. "Do you actually have any idea why I left Waynesville so suddenly? I will bet that you do not ... almost nobody knows the real story."

I simply waited.

"It was 1958," he began. "You know that *Brown Versus the Board of Education* came down from the Supreme Court in 1954, but, most states were not voluntarily integrating schools until the courts pressured them. Integration was talked about in Haywood County, but, as far as we knew, any real move toward inclusion was not in the works.

"You remember that we were having August band practice once a week the month before school started. We did so every year. The High School band was getting their first halftime show for the opening football game the first weekend after school started. I always started practice for the eighth-grade band then so you would get it in your heads that this is what we did before you got to High School the next year." I was right with him, remembering that we felt like we were big kids getting to have weekly band practice a month before school started.

Mr. Campbell went on. He was not looking at me but was looking far away. It was as if he had moved back in time as his story unfolded. "We had had one weekly practice and we were back for our second week. I remember we were working on the "Our Director" march since the eighth-grade band would be marching in the Labor Day Parade in Canton and the Apple Festival Parade in Hendersonville on Labor Day.

"Right in the middle of our practice, Mr. Bowles, the Superintendent, marched in the door of the band building and interrupted our practice." I remembered this part very well. Mr. Bowles had interrupted practice, and he and Mr. Campbell had had a sort of florid but private talk, after which Mr. Bowles stomped out of the room, and Mr. Campbell sent us home.

"So, here's what happened. None of us teachers had yet received our contracts for the coming year. This was very unusual since we usually had them and signed them at the end of the previous year. Nobody really thought anything about it though. There was very little teacher turnover in Haywood County.

"Mr. Bowles had my contract for the new year in his hand. He handed it to me and then gave me his instructions. He wanted me to ask him if the schools were going to integrate and then to refuse to sign my contract so that if integration was ordered they could simply shut the schools down because they had no teachers.

"I told him where he could stuff the contract and that I would have nothing to do with a scheme like that. He told me that my time in Haywood County was over and stomped out of the room. When I got to my office, I found my contract torn to pieces and stuffed under the door.

"I already had three job offers from places that I had not initiated ... they had come to me. One of them was in Glendale, California. I got on the phone and took the job. Before it was totally dark that night, everything I owned was in the trunk of my Plymouth and I was headed to California. I did have to ship the motorbike out there, though." And that was the end of the story.

We finished our dinner and headed out to the library for my storytelling program. When we got there, Mr. Campbell knew most of the audience since he was such a regular volunteer after his retirement from teaching. He had moved from Glendale to be the band director in Bakersfield years earlier.

I was introduced by the librarian and proceeded to tell stories for about ninety minutes. All this time Mr. Campbell was sitting in his front-row seat, reacting as though he and I had been best friends for his entire life!

When I finished the formal part of the program, I decided to do something highly personal while I still had the attention of the audience. I wanted to give that audience, most of whom already knew my old band director as either a library volunteer or a retired school teacher, a little more insight into the person I had known all those years ago. So, I told them about my experience as his seventh-grade student. I told about making first chair trumpet and lessons we had all learned from that experience, lessons that I carried with me my entire life. I told them how he taught us about being not just on time but early for every engagement, a lesson that I still follow and value to this very day. As I was telling them about how his high expectations pulled a level of effort from us that could not have been achieved any other way, I glanced at Mr. Campbell and saw that his head was in his arms and he was crying. I quickly finished my little elegy, thanked everyone for coming, and the audience departed.

As soon as everyone was gone, Mr. Campbell came over to me and began to apologize. "I'm sorry I got carried away while you were talking there at the end," he started. "Here's what happened. You see, if I had actually remembered who you were when you said all those things about me, I might not have been affected in that way. But when a little boy whom I did not even remember began to tell people that years ago I did something as a teacher that had lasting positive meaning in his life, it was too much to bear. I guess you told me why I spent my life as a teacher, not for those I remember, but for all those children I might have taught something whom I cannot honestly say that I remember. Thank you!" He did something I would never have expected from that old teacher: he gave me a big hug and we both cried a little bit more.

Mr. Campbell and I kept up with one another from then on after that event. He had a caravan camper in Australia, where he spent about half of each year traveling around by himself. He had adopted two former students who had no families of support and sent both to college. Some years later he moved from California to a retirement community in Northern Virginia where he could live out his days closer to one of the young men he had adopted. He took care of himself and moved into his nineties in excellent health.

In the spring of 2020, at age ninety-four and still in excellent health, Mr. Bob Campbell contracted COVID-19. The demon virus had slipped its way into the retirement community where he lived. The virus ambushed my old teacher and won the battle; Mr. Campbell became one of the Coronavirus's early statistics.

Now that he is gone, I must tell his story more than ever. It is the story of what it means to spend a life giving to others and doing what is right ... even when you never know what you have done and get no credit for it. I am just glad that, on one evening in Bakersfield, I could, in front of others, give him a bit of credit for giving me a better life.

Chapter Eight

Corporal Pritchard Smith

IN THE EIGHTH GRADE, I was in Mr. Roy Haupt's room. He was my first male teacher and a genius in many ways.

One Friday in the fall of the year he gave us an assignment for the weekend. This was not usual, and, as he explained, we might need a Saturday and a Sunday to get the assignment lined up and completed. This was the assignment: we were to interview an adult about their job and then prepare an oral report to present in class the following week.

At first, this sounded like it would be an easy assignment, but then I started wondering who I might interview. Being introverted, it was not easy for me to think about going up to any adult and asking them if I might ask them questions about their work and life. Most of the adults I knew were relatives, and they all had what I considered to be profoundly boring jobs.

My mama was a schoolteacher, as were all six of her sisters

and many of their husbands. My granddaddy was a farmer, and he was also not a person I could ever talk with. Daddy worked at the bank, and his job had to do with arithmetic, so it had to be very boring. My Uncle Grover was a lawyer in town and that did not sound interesting at all to me. The only relative who had an interesting job was my Uncle Jim, who was a chemist. Unfortunately, he and Aunt Nancy lived in Morristown, Tennessee—two and a half hours away. To save myself, I could not figure out who I was going to interview.

I thought about this all Friday afternoon and evening. I had a hard time going to sleep that night. The assignment was holding up all of my thoughts.

On Saturday I just pretended that I didn't have an assignment so the day would not be completely ruined. Late Saturday morning we all went to town to go shopping for winter clothing. When the shopping was finished, we stopped at Charlie's Drive-In for lunch before returning home.

The ride home from Charlie's was less than two miles. Daddy drove up the long hill past the hospital and down the other side past the Drive-In Theatre. Up to the hospital, the speed limit was twenty miles per hour as we were still in town. But, as we started down the hill toward the Theatre, we left the city limits, and the speed limit went up to thirty-five until around the curve past our house where it became fifty-five from there all the way to Lake Junaluska.

As we drove down the straight stretch heading for our

driveway where it turned up the hill to our house, Daddy suddenly said, "Look there ... there's a 'Whammy!'" We looked where he was pointing and saw what looked like two small black rubber hoses stretched across the road in front of us. They appeared to be maybe ten yards apart.

"What's a 'Whammy?'" Mama asked just as my brother, Joe, and I were thinking the same thing.

Daddy explained, "It's what they call a speed trap." He pointed up the road that went to the Leatherwood's house just as we passed it. There, partly hidden, was a North Carolina Highway Patrol car.

"See," he went on, "When your car goes over those two cords, they send a signal up to the Patrol car. It measures the time it took your car from hitting the first one to hitting the second one and that tells the Patrolman how fast you were going. When drivers come around the curve here after going fifty-five, they tend to forget to slow down when the speed limit drops to thirty-five. He's out raising money for the State of North Carolina."

In that moment, I thought, that's not all he's doing. He's sitting right there waiting to be interviewed for my assignment for Roy Haupt!

When we got out of the car at home, I announced that I needed to work on a school assignment. I got my little notebook and headed out the back door of our house and across the yard to the Leatherwood's house. Down their driveway and off to the left was the silver and black North Carolina Highway Patrol car. It was clearly visible from here but almost totally hidden from traffic passing on the highway below. I could see a large black cord running up the side of the road from the highway. This was certainly part of the "whammy" Daddy was talking about.

I walked around to the side of the car so that the Patrolman would see me before I surprised him. The car was a new 1958 Ford. It had a whip antenna on the back, and, in those days, a single red light encased in chrome on the roof of the car. I waved to the Patrolman, and he waved back to me. With that signal of acceptance, I walked up to the driver's side of the car, where he sat with the window rolled down.

"Hello," I shyly started. "My name is Donald Davis. I live right up there," as I pointed back toward our house.

"Well, Donald Davis, you must be Joe Davis's boy. I am Corporal Pritchard Smith. I have a girl about your age ... her name is Linda Kay Smith. Do you know her from school?"

"I know who she is," I answered. "She is a little older than I am, so I don't actually know her person to person." This was good. If this man had a daughter about my age, he would understand having school assignments and would probably agree to help me.

"I have a question," I went on. "I am in Mr. Roy Haupt's room in the eighth grade and our assignment for the weekend is to interview someone about their job and make a report on it next week. I was wondering if I could interview you?"

He smiled, "Climb in the back seat. Linda Kay was also in Mr. Haupt's room, and she had to do assignments like that. I'll be glad to try to help you out but being a Patrolman is probably not as interesting as you think it is. A lot of time is spent driving around or waiting on an assignment like this," he pointed to the box on the dash of the car that was connected with the cord through the open window.

"It would help me," I said, "If you would tell me about how this thing works. My Daddy says it is called the 'whammy.'"

He chuckled. "I've heard that people call it that. They even call getting caught for speeding like this is 'getting the whammy put on you.'"

He began to explain to me all about how the speed detector worked like Daddy had said, by measuring the time between when a car hits the first cord until the time when it hits the second cord. Cars below us would cross the "whammy" and their speed would light up on the screen of the box on the dash of the Patrol car. We watched for a few minutes: thirty-six ... forty ... twenty-eight ... thirty-four ... thirty-five ... all acceptable as the speed limit there was thirty-five miles per hour.

"You see," he went on, "Right around that curve below your house the speed limit is fifty-five. Right about where your driveway is it drops to thirty-five. Then, up at the top of the

127

hill above the Drive-In, you come to the city limits, and there the speed limit drops to twenty. What happens is that a lot of people heading for town don't slow down enough when the speed limit drops to thirty-five and then they go roaring into town too fast for safety. We're not giving a lot of tickets unless somebody is way over, but I do give a lot of warnings to teach people to learn to slow down on this stretch of highway." I was trying to write all of this down as he explained it.

The two of us sat there watching cars and checking their speeds for a while and he told me more things I could put in my interview report. He told me that in North Carolina what most people called the Highway Patrol was actually the State Patrol and that they had authority everywhere in North Carolina except military bases and Indian reservations.

Corporal Smith told me that he had been offered a promotion from Corporal to Sergeant, but, if he took it, he would have to move to a different district and away from Waynesville. He turned the promotion down, he said, because his family liked living in Waynesville. He said he didn't want Linda Kay to have to move to a new school and leave all of her friends. He really was a very nice man and easy to be with.

No cars had been speeding the whole time we were talking. Then, all of a sudden, both of us heard a car coming before we even saw it. It was not coming in toward town but was leaving town heading toward Lake Junaluska. When the car came into first view, I saw that it was a 1950 Oldsmobile. It had no hubcaps and there was a lot of Bondo and primer paint on it. It must have had what my Mama called "gutted-out mufflers" since it was making a loud roaring sound. It was also moving very fast!

The Oldsmobile hit the whammy cord running wide open. Suddenly, the number "sixty-seven" came up on the speed box on the dash, and, in that moment, Corporal Smith totally forgot that I was in the back seat. He jerked the Ford into gear and, at the same time, tossed the connection cord out the window, and we were on the way in full pursuit of the speeding, rough-looking car.

The siren was blaring, and I knew that the red light on top of the car had to be flashing too. We rounded the curve and passed the driveway that went up to our house. About that time Corporal Smith realized that he had an eighth-grade boy in the back seat of his patrol car! "Get down, Davis," he said. "You're not supposed to be in here! Don't let anybody see you. Your daddy would kill both of us if he knew this was happening." Now we were in hot pursuit, and there was nothing for him to do but finish what was started.

The Oldsmobile flew by the Health Department and Ed Sims' Store. I was peeping over the seat and saw that we were going seventy-five miles an hour chasing the jalopy. We were gaining on the car, but it was not starting to slow down at all. By the time we passed the Welch Farm Place I could see that the car was weaving all over the road. "Stay down, Davis," Corporal Smith ordered, "It looks like he's drunk!"

At about that time, the pursued car started around the curve just past the back end of Howell Mill Road. The obviously-intoxicated driver misjudged the curve and went off into the ditch on the right-hand side. Still running wide open, the car cleaned out the ditch for twenty yards until the driver jerked the steering wheel to the left. When it came out of the ditch, the car went almost straight across the highway, down a bank, across a small field, and ended up with its front end in a little creek.

By then, Corporal Smith had stopped the Patrol car. As he jumped out the door, continuing the pursuit on foot, he yelled to me, "Go up there in the woods, Davis. Get you a good hiding place and stay there until I come back to get you. Nobody needs to know anything about this little adventure!"

I crawled out of the right side of the parked car, clambered up a small bank, and found a safe place where I could be hidden and, at the same time, watch what was happening below.

Corporal Smith followed the path the car had taken. Down where the Oldsmobile had ended up, he disappeared from my vision. I couldn't see him for a few minutes. Then he emerged from the little creek into the field. Corporal Smith restrained a staggering man. With one hand, the officer held his captive by the back of his belt, and with the other hand, Smith held the man's shirt at the back of his neck. I could see that the man was hand-cuffed and was so intoxicated that he could not have walked without Corporal Smith mostly carrying him.

About a half-dozen steps behind them, there followed another man. This one was walking on his own, but he was shaking, and his pants were totally soaked down the front like he had wet himself. I later learned that he was a hitchhiker who had been picked up by the drunk driver, and he had, indeed, wet his pants. He was so scared.

The wet-pants man shook his head when it looked like Corporal Smith was offering him a ride back to town and started walking on his own like he was finished with riding in cars for a while. At the same time, the Corporal deposited the drunk in the back seat of the Patrol car, which he turned around right in the middle of the highway and headed back toward town.

I could have walked back home as it was not a mile away, but I had been told to stay here. If Corporal Smith came back for me and I was not where he left me, what would he have done then? He might have come to my house to be sure I was okay and then we would have both been found out. I figured I better stay and have some story ready for my parents about where I had been for so long. I could truthfully tell them that I had just been working on a school assignment.

I didn't have a watch, so I had no idea about how long

it was until Corporal Smith came back. I saw him pull the Patrol car off to the side of the road below me. He tooted the horn, and I slid down the little bank and hopped back into the car. He didn't even have to tell me to stay down as he turned around and slowly drove back up to where I had gotten in the car to begin with. On the way, he told me that he had to take the drunk man to jail and make arrangements to get the wrecked car towed in.

When I got out of the car all I could do was say, "Thank you!" with no reference to what I was thanking him for. When he said, "You're welcome," there was also no clear reference. I walked home to our house without looking back.

I was a little bit shaky when I went into the house. Both my parents were sitting in the living room watching television. My Daddy looked up and he was the one to ask, "Did you get your assignment done?" I had already thought about this.

"I got most of it done," I started, "But, there is one more thing I need some help with. I am supposed to interview someone this weekend about their job and make a report on it in Mr. Haupt's class this week. I was wondering if I could interview you about your job at the bank? I think that would be very interesting to my class."

And that is exactly what I did.

Chapter Nine

Old Slick

FROM THE FIRST-GRADE THROUGH THE SIXTH-GRADE, all of my friends were either friends from school or friends from the Methodist Church. So, my school friends were limited to students at Hazelwood School.

When I got to the seventh grade the world exploded. Now I was in school with students who had spent their elementary years not only at Hazelwood but also at East Waynesville, Central Elementary, Lake Junaluska, and Maggie Elementary schools. It was a new world of friends.

Right there, in the seventh grade, I joined the band, and from the start, all my lifelong friends were fellow band students. There was Bill McInvaille, Doug Robertson, Freddie Hall, and David Morgan. David was my instant best friend, and gradually, we realized that, including school and band, we spent more time together than either of us spent with our families.

At the same time, when I graduated from Hazelwood Elementary to Waynesville Junior High School, our family also moved to the other side of town. This just happened to be the same side of town where David and Bill and Doug and Freddie lived. This meant that, instead of my old Boy Scout troop back in Hazelwood, I was now not only in band but also in the same Scout troop with all of them: Troop 3, Waynesville.

We all loved Boy Scouts for one reason: camping! Forget all of the merit badges related to first aid, swimming, and plant identification, our dedication to Boy Scouts was all about hiking, cooking, and sleeping in the woods. This got us away from home and enabled us to talk all night about everything on the face of the earth and beyond. Camping was not just something we did, it was who we were in our deepest hearts.

By the time we got to the end of the seventh grade, we had about given up Boy Scouts in favor of just going camping on our own. There were many places to go, living in a county in which more than half the land was Great Smoky Mountains National Park, Blue Ridge Parkway, and Pisgah National Forest. Besides that, there were the farms where my mother and father had grown up that were totally available to us.

It was during the beginning of the school year in the eighth grade, and I was over at David's house one day when his Uncle Don and Aunt Mary Jean came by. Mary Jean's father was Mr. Homer West who owned both the land where he and Uncle Don farmed and all of Big Stomp Mountain above

Ratcliffe Cove.

We were all talking about how much we loved to go hiking and camping when suddenly Aunt Mary Jean offered, "Boys, you know that Daddy owns all of Big Stomp, and up there on the mountain, there is an old fox hunting cabin that he and some of his friends built back in the thirties. I don't think he's been up there for maybe ten years. I'll talk to him and see if it's okay with him for you boys to go and camp up there in the old cabin. Nobody else is using it."

This turned out to be a magical day for all of us. Little did we know how much we would come to love this mountain and this little old cabin. Our adventures were about to start.

My Mama had to check with David's Aunt Mary Jean before she would give me approval to go, but, after that telephone call, all was clear. The plan was that on the following Thursday, after school, David, Bill, and I would meet at my house, pack all of our stuff, and put it in the trunk of Mama's car. That way, she could pick us up at school at the end of the day on Friday and take us straight out to Mr. West's house where we would get the key and have a good start at hiking up to the cabin. We would stop at Ratcliffe Cove Grocery on the way and get our food ... mostly hot dogs.

When the next Friday came, we were all packed and loaded. None of the three of us had any idea what happened at school that day; all we were doing was daydreaming about the upcoming camping trip. We just grinned at each other every time we passed all day long. At last, the sixth-period bell rang, and we gathered in front of the band building to wait for Mama's car.

Pretty soon the green Plymouth arrived. We all jumped in the back seat to be chauffeured. "Do you think you have all your stuff, boys?" She asked us.

"All but our food," I answered. "We've got our saved-up money. If you will just stop at the little grocery store in Ratcliffe Cove, we can run in and get our groceries."

"Oh, I'll go with you. I'll be glad to pay for your food."

"Oh, no, Mrs. Davis," David quickly jumped in. "We all brought our money. My grandmother wouldn't be happy if she knew you paid for our food. We will be quick... You just stay in the car." The reason for all of this was that one of the items on our shopping list was Swisher Sweets cigars and we knew that we wouldn't be able to get our necessary cigars if Mama came into the store.

The stop was made, the shopping was done, and soon we pulled into the driveway at Mr. West's house. Aunt Mary Jean had told David to knock on the back door, and Mr. West would give us the key to the padlock on the cabin. Mama told us goodbye *several* times and warned us to be careful *more times than that*. We happily watched her drive away, leaving us with our packs in the side yard of the West's house.

All three of us went up to the back door carrying our

backpacks with us. David knocked on the door, it opened, and there stood Mr. West. He was quite old and slightly decrepit-looking. I remembered Daddy saying that people called him "Old Slick" and I couldn't imagine that nickname going with the old man standing in front of us.

Mr. West knew David, of course. David introduced Bill and me and tried to make some family connections for us that Mr. West would recognize. Then we reminded him of why we were there and asked if we could have the key.

"Well, boys, I've been thinking about that. I haven't been up to the old cabin in a long time, so, this first time, I just thought I would go with you boys. We can even take my old Jeep, so you boys won't have to walk or carry all this stuff. David, you can drive." (We were all thirteen years old.)

About that time, Mrs. West came into the room. "You boys take care of the old man," was all she said to us before she walked back out, and we did not see her again.

He picked up an old Duxback hunting coat and slipped it on. The pockets of this old coat held everything he took with him on the trip. "Let's go out to the barn and get the Jeep, boys." We had very mixed feelings. We did not want this old man to go with us, but at the same time, getting to take the Jeep with David driving was going to add to our adventure.

We got out to the barn where an old, green, Jeep CJ-5 awaited us patiently under the shed. Mr. West got David to start the Jeep and back it out. It smelled like a wonderful combination of dirt and motor oil.

In the back of the Jeep was a large homemade dog crate covered with chicken wire. "We're going to take my two foxhounds with us, boys. They'll entertain us with their singing tonight if they can get on a good trail." Then he got two Walker hounds out of a pen and put them in the dog crate. "I'm going to take my little pet with me too," Mr. West remarked as he rounded up a little feisty half-sized terrier-of-a-dog and held it in his lap as he crawled in the passenger seat of the Jeep.

There was now nowhere for Bill and me to ride since the dog crate was in place of the back seat. "Just stand back there on the tow bar, boys, and hold on to the bar under the back of the canvas top. You'll be fine!" With those instructions, we tossed our backpacks in beside the dog crate, jumped on the back following his instructions, and we were off!

The route up the mountain to the cabin started out following a very flat farm road that ran along the side of a pasture paralleling a little creek. It was an easy, smooth ride and gave Bill and me a chance to get used to our riding arrangement while David drove the Jeep. Even at age thirteen, we all knew how to drive from being around farm equipment and being recruited to help on many occasions. Mr. West was happy with David's driving.

At the top of the pasture, we reached a place where the road made a ford through the little creek we had been following.

The road dipped down into and through the stream. Bill and I came out with wet feet on the other side. The back end of the Jeep had dipped under the water as we crossed. The dogs all seemed to be enjoying the ride as they panted and looked around to watch the scenery along the way.

The road now began to wind up the mountain and into the woodland. We crawled along in low gear, not really going any faster than we could have walked, but free of the burden of having to carry anything.

Soon the road came to a washed-out section where another high-up creek actually ran down the center of the road itself. The water had washed out all the dirt through the years and the road that was left was totally made of the rocks that were left. David shifted into low-range four-wheel-drive and put the Jeep into low gear, and we crawled more slowly than ever, listening to the little four-cylinder engine roar.

Finally, we came out into a large stand of hemlock trees through which the road passed. On the other side of the hemlocks, we arrived at the cabin.

There was a large flat section of land here, all covered with lovely hardwoods. In the middle of this open forest stood the little cabin. It was made of poplar logs chinked with old cement and was about sixteen-by-twenty-four feet with a smaller room sticking out on one side in the back that we assumed must be the kitchen. The tin roof had an aged patina of rust.

"Here we are, boys," intoned Mr. West. "Let's get the door unlocked, and you can put your stuff inside. I'll let the dogs out of the crate and put them in their pen." There was a large, fenced dog lot on the lower side of the cabin.

David, Bill, and I got our backpacks out of the Jeep and followed Mr. West up onto the little porch and to the solid front door. Mr. West reached into his pockets to find the key. We watched him search one pocket and then the next until he had gone through his pants and his coat two or three times.

"Now I remember," he said. "I left that old key hanging on a nail in the kitchen cabinet. It's still there! Get back on the Jeep, boys. We'll have to go back and get it."

He did secure the dogs in the dog pen, and then all four of us remounted the Jeep. We headed all the way back down the mountain to his house so Mr. West could get the forgotten key.

When we got down to the house, Mrs. West was sitting in a rocking chair out on the side porch waiting for us. "I knew you'd forget it," she started. "I looked in that cabinet as soon as you were gone, and there it was ... now here it is," she chuckled as she held the missing key out to her husband. "I hope you didn't forget anything else!" Then we headed back up the mountain.

On this return trip, David had learned the road much better, and it did not take us quite as long to get back to the cabin. Mr. West did not have to tell him anything about how to drive this time.

We all got down from the Jeep and, once again, followed Mr. West up on the porch and to the door. He had just started to get the now-recovered key from his pocket when he suddenly stopped and said, "You know, boys, I have an extra key hidden right up here in a crack over the door just in case I ever forget to bring one. He pulled down the now-remembered hidden key and used it to unlock the padlock, never even pulling the one we had made the trip to get out of his pocket. We were beginning to learn what a weekend with Old Slick was going to be like.

Inside the old cabin, there was a large rock fireplace filling most of the end to the left of the door. In front of the fireplace was a wooden table with four cane-bottom chairs pulled up around it. Arranged around the other end of this one large room were three beds, two single and one double, against the far end wall and under the only window in the place.

Mr. West went over to one of the beds and lifted the edge of the covers, revealing ancient, yellowed sheets topped with equally old-looking blankets. "See, boys, you didn't even need to bring your sleeping bags since these beds are all made up and ready to sleep in."

Yeah, I thought, *these beds were probably made up in nineteen-thirty and have never been changed since then.* All three of us were relieved we had our sleeping bags to keep us safely enclosed on top of the covers.

Next, the beds were assigned. Mr. West claimed the single bed next to the back wall. He pointed Bill to the other single bed along the front wall. David and I were consigned to share the double bed under the window at the end. The three of us soon gave these beds names. Bill's bed we named "The Valley of Fatigue," our double bed David and I called "The Honeymoon Couch," and Mr. West's bed—in which he actually slept under the old covers—we named "The Bug Bench," since we saw a layer of bug carcasses lining the sheets when he turned the covers back to get in.

Now that sleeping arrangements were made, it was time to turn to plans for supper. We had brought plenty of hot dogs to share, and we invited Old Slick to have hot dogs with us. At that time, he began to pull loose eggs out of the pockets of the Duxback coat and lay them on the table. There were a dozen eggs in all once they were all out. "Mama told me she boiled some of these," he commented and began to crack eggs, trying to find the boiled ones. Discovering that every single egg was raw, he stated, "I must not have picked up the right ones." He then used his hand to scrape the raw eggs into a pan and told us he would save them for breakfast! All we did after that was be sure that we washed the tabletop thoroughly.

With the fire built, we feasted on hot dogs that we cooked on sticks over the fire. By now, anything we might have eaten would have been delicious as were our hot dogs. The Kool-Aid we had brought to drink was as good as the hot dogs.

142

After cleaning up from eating, we noticed that it was fully dark outside and about time to settle down for bed. Mr. West had other ideas. "Boys, let's go out and feed the fox dogs. Then we can let them run a little bit." From a large barrel of dog food in the corner of the cabin, we took a good bit out for each of the fox hounds and left a dish full for the little terrier to eat in the house while we were gone.

As soon as Suke and Worley, the hounds, finished eating, Mr. West announced that we were going to let them run "so they could make some music for us." He gave them their instructions just as if they understood every word he was saying, and the dogs took off like they knew exactly where they were going. We all headed back inside and settled on the beds to await the big barking show.

In no time, the two foxhounds were on a scent—barking their heads off and going around the side of the mountain. Mr. West sat still on his bed and held one hand up to cup his ear. "What's happened to the dogs?" he asked us. "They ought to be on to something by now. I can't hear a thing!" We realized then that he was as deaf as a metal post, and all the barking in the world would make no impression on him.

Bill calmly walked over and sat down on the bed beside him. They sat there side by side with the little terrier lap dog nuzzling both of them. All of a sudden, Bill pulled the little dog's tail and the dog went, "Yap!"

Old Slick was almost on his feet with excitement. "There

they go, boys! I can hear 'em now. They are getting on a trail. I bet they're over by Windy Field. Bill kept pinching the little dog and tugging on its tail to keep it barking right in Mr. West's ear. He thought that he heard his dogs running until Bill gave out and we all settled down to sleep for the night. When we awakened the next morning, the foxhounds would be back at the cabin and asleep on the porch.

In the morning, we explored the little kitchen on the back of the cabin. It had a neat little wood stove and plenty of pots and pans. We had brought pancake mix, bacon, and syrup since David's Aunt Mary Jean had filled him in about the little kitchen. We made a big batch of pancakes and had a wonderful breakfast shared with Mr. West himself.

After we got everything all cleaned up, he said, "Let's go exploring, boys. David, you drive, and we'll all go in the Jeep." He fed the returned foxhounds, locked them in their pen, and left the terrier to sleep while we were gone. That little dog needed its rest since it had worked hard the night before and would likely have to work again in the coming evening.

Sometime early in the century, in the logging era, the mountain had been logged over. While the trees had had a half-century to grow back, the old logging roads were, though grown up somewhat, still passable with the Jeep. Mr. West gave the directions, and we explored all over the western side of Big Stomp Mountain, the half that he owned.

Finally he said, "Let's go on up to the top, boys. I haven't been up there for a while." David drove the Jeep up the winding road until it ran out at the bottom of the pastureland that covered the top of the mountain. Then Mr. West directed him to drive right up through the pasture until we ended up at the top of the mountain.

David had been driving uphill and Bill and I had been hanging onto the back of the Jeep, so, we did not know what the view was going to be like until David stopped the Jeep, and we all got out. What we saw just about took our breath away. When we turned around and looked down from the top of the mountain, there spread out below us was the entire town of Waynesville. We were, at a distance, looking right up Main Street. We could follow Main Street from the Presbyterian Church to the Baptist Church. We could all locate our houses. We could easily identify schools, the hospital, gas stations, stores, and Charlie's Restaurant. We could never have imagined that you could, from here, look down on our entire childhood world. It was magic.

"You ought to come back up here at night," Old Slick said with emotion in his voice. "That's when it is really something to see." An eventual plan was made.

We drove back down to the cabin after that and ate another round of hot dogs for lunch. We had brought enough hot dogs to get us through the entire weekend. Why try anything more complicated?

After our lunch, everyone fell asleep for a while. I never ever took a daytime nap at home, but, here, in the quiet and without agenda or responsibility, napping was the most natural thing in the world.

That night for supper, we again had hot dogs. And, once again, the fox hounds trailed a fox, and the little dog barked for Mr. West. When Sunday morning arrived, there was time for breakfast before we headed back down the mountain.

As we rode back down the old road with David driving, Mr. West said, "Well, boys, we now know that David can drive the Jeep just fine. And we know that all of you boys can handle staying at the cabin just fine. So, here's the deal: I'm going to give David the key, and you boys can come up here and stay in the cabin whenever you want to, you don't even have to ask me since I might not even be at home when you want to go. And you know where this old Jeep lives, back there in the barn. The key is always in it. I don't see why you can't use it as well. I'm glad somebody is using the old cabin after all this time." We boys were thrilled!

We could not believe it! People could call Mr. West "Old Slick" all they wanted to. This was about the greatest thing that had ever happened to us. From now on we had a way to escape from our families and go camping in a great place at the same time. We started making plans on the spot to spend all the time possible up at the cabin.

The very next weekend we planned to take our first un-chaperoned trip to the cabin, with the Jeep included.

On Thursday we packed all our stuff in the trunk of my Mama's car. With the Jeep to use, there was no limit to what we took with us. After school Friday she picked us up and took us out to the little grocery store. We let her buy the groceries for us this time since we already had our unused cigars from the weekend before. This time we also got a variety of mostly canned food instead of eating only hot dogs for the entire weekend.

She let us out at the West's house, and we headed back to the old barn to get the Jeep. With no dogs in tow, we took the dog box out of the back and installed the back seat. This gave us all room to ride while leaving plenty of room for our stuff. Then we headed up the mountain.

David was the driver. We figured he was the one Mr. West wanted to be the driver after last weekend. But, David promised that we would each get a turn when we were way up on the mountain where no one would know the difference. Bill rode in the front with David, and I stood on the drawbar on the back, holding to the top frame since this was a lot more fun than sitting in the back seat. Every moment of this new freedom was delicious.

We had checked carefully to ensure we had the key before starting out. We didn't want to waste time making an extra trip back down the mountain the way we did the weekend before. Once at the cabin, we were instantly inside and, in no time, had a big fire in the fireplace.

After our supper in front of the fire, we settled down to enjoy the evening together. We discovered playing cards and a lot of poker chips in the drawer of the wooden table in front of the fireplace. All three of us told each other that we knew how to play poker even though we really had not even a slight idea. But, despite this, we kept a big fire going and played an invented five-card game which we called poker, while we smoked our Swisher Sweets cigars around the table. David, Bill, and I were having the time of our lives.

Finally, we settled into bed and talked ourselves to sleep making plans for the coming day.

On Saturday morning we built a fire in the wood cook stove in the little kitchen and enjoyed a breakfast of pancakes. After we had cleaned everything up from this late-morning meal, we got in the Jeep and headed out to explore Big Stomp Mountain. David drove first, but eventually, he let Bill and me take turns driving. With no memory of when I did not know how to drive, taking on the Jeep at age thirteen was no difficulty at all.

We explored the old logging roads and found more places to go than we had with Mr. West the weekend before. We went everywhere except up to the top of the mountain; we were saving this for a trip in the dark later that evening.

Back at the cabin in the late afternoon, we branched

out and had advanced international cuisine for this evening's supper: Chef Boyardee canned spaghetti heated in a pan over the wood fire in the fireplace. We three got forks out of the little kitchen and sat around the wooden table, all eating straight out of the same pan.

The next day was Sunday and the day when we would have to head back down the mountain in the afternoon. Again, we made pancakes for breakfast. We then cleaned up the cabin and packed all our stuff into the Jeep. Our plan was to ride and drive around the mountain for a few hours until we knew we had to get home by late afternoon.

David was driving. When we were riding around the day before, one of the most fascinating places we had explored was a big high-mountain field David said was called "Windy Field." It was about fifteen acres and was clear of trees but grown up with thistles and milkweed. Both the milkweed and the thistles were at the conclusion of their autumn bloom and in the process of going to seed. A blend of thistledown and milkweed seeds blew across the windy field.

We drove back up to this place to look again. It was so beautiful. All of a sudden, David said: "Watch this!" He backed the Jeep up to get a good head start and then drove full speed right through the middle of the field sending clouds of flying milkweed seeds and thistledown billowing in the air all around us. We laughed and laughed when we stopped on the far side of the field.

For the following hour, the three of us took turns driving through the field over and over again. Each pass sent great billows of seeds blowing into the air until, finally, we had flattened all the thistle and milkweed plants.

As we sat there in the Jeep laughing at the show we had created we all became aware of a growing hissing noise coming from under the hood of the Jeep. We opened the hood to discover steam forcing its way out around the edges of the cap on the radiator. The Jeep was so overheated it was about to blow the cap off the radiator. At the same time, all three of us realized what had happened.

When we were having such a good time running the Jeep through the clouds of milkweed seeds and thistle down, those same seeds had blocked all the air passages through the radiator. Looking down behind the grill of the Jeep, we found a solidly impacted blanket of white fluff embedded into the front of the radiator. Being thirteen-year-old boys, what did we do? We just stood there and laughed like we had somehow pulled off a great trick.

Then we realized we had to get the Jeep back to the cabin and eventually back down the mountain. A little creek trickled just below the big field. We could hear the water tumbling from where we now stood. David took off his hat, walked down to the creek, and filled the hat with water. For the time being, this did not do us any good. The radiator was still so hot that we could not take the cap off. As the water leaked out onto the ground, we realized we were going to have to sit here and wait until the Jeep cooled off enough to take the cap off the radiator before we could add any water to it.

We sat around and talked while we waited. Finally, things cooled down, and after the cap was removed, David made a dozen trips to the creek and back carrying cold water to refill the steamed-out radiator.

We restarted the Jeep and headed back to the cabin, only to discover on arrival that the Jeep was overheated and steaming once again. The root of the problem, the stopped-up radiator core, was as blocked as ever. It was going to take a lot of work to clean it out and we could not even figure out how you would do a project like that. This was not our problem, though, as tomorrow, we would just take the Jeep back down and put it in the barn, and Old Slick would never even know what had happened!

Now it was time to head down the mountain. David spoke up: "I was thinking about it in the night," he started. If the Jeep is going to overheat on us on the way down, the best way to do it is for me to drive as fast as I can so we can get it over with. I figure this is the smartest thing to do." (This logic was coming from a future high school valedictorian!) It never occurred to any of us that we would be going downhill all the way—and except for a few brief moments when we might start the Jeep to cross level stretches—we could simply coast all the way. But high speed sounded like more fun, and by now, we had all accepted David as the Jeep commander.

We loaded up and stashed all our stuff in the back seat. Bill and I, by now, preferred to ride standing on the rear drawbar. Holding on to the rear bar, we looked out over the top of the Jeep toward the front as David drove. We also got to bounce along in what felt like a much more dangerous way. David started the Jeep, and we headed out.

He had seriously meant it when he told us he was going to drive down the mountain as fast as possible. We headed down the fairly smooth first part of the road through the hemlock trees. We slid from side to side on the hemlock needle accumulation every time there was a slight curve in the road.

The next part of the road was the washed-out section over the big rocks. He didn't seem to slow down much here and it felt like we alternated between flying into the air and hitting the bottom of the Jeep on the exposed boulders as we charged along. Bill and I were having a wonderful time hanging on and constantly bouncing into the air as we sped. Everything was so noisy that none of us could hear one another if we tried to carry on any conversation. It was just whoops and yells.

The following section of the road was actually an old logging roadbed through the woods. We made our way down toward the pasture near the bottom of the mountain. This road was very defined and narrow but more smooth and gentle, so David really built up speed here. We were coming toward a place we had noticed many times before: it was a narrowed place where a large oak tree had fallen across the road. Mr. West or some of his compatriots had used chain saws to cut out a wide enough section of the fallen log to open up the road, but there was not much spare distance on either side as you passed through. David was headed full speed toward this narrow slot without realizing something about the old Jeep.

The spare wheel and tire were mounted on the side of the Jeep on a bracket that was bolted to the body just above and behind the right rear wheel. It stuck out about ten inches from the Jeep. David was unaware of this protrusion as he aimed the Jeep through what seemed to be the center of the opening. Suddenly a loud noise accompanied the Jeep's jumping sideways against the bank on the opposite side of the road and coming to an abrupt stop. The wheel, tire, and bracket now stuck out at about a thirty-degree angle, and the body of the Jeep where it was attached was also warped. We had caught the spare wheel full speed on the solid oak log.

When we got out to see what had happened, David was the first one to laugh. Bill and I joined him because, after all, he was our thirteen-year-old leader. "What's Old Slick going to say?" I asked.

"The old man will never even notice it. We'll just back the Jeep into the barn, and by the time he sees it, he will wonder why he can't remember how it happened." We all laughed some more.

By now, we noticed that the Jeep had, in fact, come to a boil. So, we stopped there until it cooled off and replenished the radiator from the creek before finishing our trip down to the West's house and barn.

We did not stop at the house. No, David drove straight on back to the barn. We quickly unloaded everything, and then he did back the green Jeep as far into the dark and as close to the edge on the right side as he could. Standing outside, you could not see the bent wheel. We were concentrating so much on hiding this that we did not even notice all the thistle down and milkweed fragments hanging down from under the radiator. The Jeep quietly hissed as we told it goodbye.

We somehow knew that we should not try to return to the cabin the next weekend. In fact, it might have been several weeks before we got up our nerve and decided it was time to go again. Besides, even if Old Slick had discovered the Jeep, we figured he would have had it fixed and forgotten all about it by now. So, the plan was made. On the next Thursday, we loaded all our stuff in my Mama's car so she could take us out to the West's house the next day to begin our weekend adventure.

She let us out in the driveway, and we picked up our packs and slipped by the house back toward the old barn. We hoped to get the Jeep and take off before being spotted by Old Slick. All was well, no one seemed to be around the house anywhere. Then we rounded the corner and were at the barn.

The green Jeep was no longer parked far back in the barn.

No, it was now pulled out beside the barn, and leaning back in a cane-bottom chair propped against the front bumper was Mr. Homer West himself. We never came to know whether, by keeping up with David's Uncle Don or Aunt Mary Jean, he was being informed about when we were going to be there or whether he had been sitting out there every Friday afternoon on his own, just waiting until we decided to come back.

"Well, hello, boys!" he started. "I was wondering when you would be coming back. I'm pleased to see all of you." We had nothing to say. He continued.

"Seems like you boys did quite a job on my Jeep. Yes sir, you did. I've had to go to a lot of trouble and spend a little bit of money since I've seen you last. All that thistledown and milkweed.... That must have come out of Windy Field. There's not that much anywhere else that I know of. It must have been a lot of fun at the time. I got the Jeep towed up to Clayton Walker's Esso, and Little Red, who works up there, spent most of a day with a compressed air hose blowing it all out."

He went on, "Back when I did that to my daddy's first John Deere tractor, I had to spend longer than that poking it all out by hand with a piece of baling wire 'cause we didn't have any compressed air back them. But this time it cost me twenty dollars.

"And then there was that tire business. Did you know that you busted the spare and also bent the rim? And also bent the mounting bracket at the same time? I had to go over to Betsy Schulhofer's junk yard and get a new bracket off of another old Jeep and buy another rim from her also. That was another thirteen dollars. Then it was another five dollars back at the Esso station getting a used tire for a new spare, plus a dollar for a tube and mounting everything. Then there was the gas and my time.

"Boys," he was not interested in stopping until he had had his say, "You know what most people call me? 'Old Slick.' Do you know there's a reason for that? I don't need to explain it to you because you can figure it out with regard to yourselves in this moment. But, let me say that I am eighty-three years old, and I have a seventy-year head start on you boys. All of the smart things that you think you are the first ones to think up ... about all of those things, I not only thought up but tried out and learned my lesson from *before your parents were even born*. There's just no way you can catch up!

"Why boys," he went on, "One time back when this road was not paved and didn't even have any gravel on it, it was just dust and dirt, Old Man Ratcliffe, up around that curve, had a whole bunch of Rhode Island Red chickens that hung out in the road. They liked to fluff up the dust and have chicken dust baths. I was driving our old Model T truck up the road, and when I came around the curve, all those chickens were in the road. Instead of slowing down as they tried to fly up in the air and get out of the way, with my undeveloped brain, I decided that the thing to do was to see how many of them I could hit with the truck. You boys think that running through thistledown and milkweed made a mess! You should have seen that Model T when I got home with feathers, blood, feet, and chicken guts hanging all over the front. I had to work after school for a week for Old Man Ratcliffe for every chicken I had killed, and he was the one who told my daddy how many he had lost. I also got a big whooping at home.

"You see, boys, you are just small-time operators over against Old Slick. Now, here is what we are going to do. You boys are going to keep on going up to the cabin just like you wanted to; I expect you to go up there at least once a month. But, no Jeep. No, from now on, you are going to have to walk up there and carry all your stuff with you, one trip for every two dollars I had to spend putting the Jeep back in order. It was close to forty dollars, so that brings us to twenty weekends."

Right then, we knew we were all going to do this. There was too much liability in having any of our parents learn what had happened and living with the consequences. So, for the next year, we carried all our stuff to the cabin. We didn't even count the weeks since we knew that Old Slick himself would be keeping track.

One day in the spring of the year, we showed up for our weekend trip, and he was sitting out on the porch waiting for us. "Come up here, boys." We obeyed. "This is too nice of a day to walk. I know you've only made about a dozen trips since we started our deal, but you've all learned your lesson." He reached out and handed David the Jeep keys. We apologized again for what we had done, thanked him profusely, and, after loading up, David drove carefully and slowly up the mountain to the cabin.

From then on through high school, we always got to use the Jeep to go to the cabin. Not only did we use it, we voluntarily took care of it. We made sure that it was always left full of gas, that the antifreeze was checked and adequate, that the tires were inflated properly, and that the oil was changed and the chassis was greased regularly. I am sure that Old Slick won much more than he lost in the end.

We have a grandson named Frank. Frank was born when I was seventy years old. He is a very clever boy, but sometimes, as I watch him inventing and exploring the world, I feel a little bit sorry for him. After all, I have a seventy-year head start on him! I watch him make what he believes to be unique discoveries and I smile. But, I want him to keep up with his discoveries, and, by the time he gets to be thirteen, maybe he will learn enough even to call me "Old Slick."

Chapter Ten

Coach Weatherby

CARLTON E. WEATHERBY WAS THE HEAD FOOTBALL COACH at Waynesville Township High School from 1930 until 1956. After he retired as football coach, he remained in his other long-time position as principal of Waynesville Junior and Senior High School. He was principal throughout my tenure there, from seventh grade through high school graduation.

Waynesville Township High School was one large campus. There was one building called the Junior High School Building that housed all the classrooms for the seventh and eighth grades. It also had its own gym.

The other buildings were the Band Building, housing space for Junior and Senior High School bands, chorus, and orchestra. Then there was the old main building and the new science building. The new building also held the cafeteria and the main gymnasium. Everyone in the seventh through twelfth grades shared both the lunchroom and the school library in the old building.

There were probably about twelve hundred students in all when I was there, and Coach Weatherby (as he was still called long after retiring as football coach) ran the entire school. There was no assistant principal because he did not need one. He and Mrs. Mary Fisher in the office were the total administrative staff. They dealt with academics, school buses, special activities, teacher issues, attendance, health concerns, and everything related to discipline.

I first encountered Coach Weatherby as a school disciplinarian when I was in the ninth grade, my first official year in high school. We were in Mr. Bill Swift's boys' health and physical education class when it happened. It was a cold winter day, and Mr. Swift, who, in his defense, had no hair to keep his head warm, decided that it was too cold for him to go outside for P.E. So, he stayed in his classroom while he sent all of us boys outside to run laps around the football field for the fifty-minute class period.

Who got the idea? I do not know, but someone in the class pulled out a pack of cigarettes. It was a full pack, so there were enough cigarettes for every student in the class. When the cigarettes were passed out, we all lit up. Then we proceeded to run laps around the field while we puffed on cigarettes at the same time.

We did not realize how much time had passed when Mr.

Swift came outside to tell us that we could come back into the building. He discovered all of us boldly puffing away. We were told to keep the cigarettes in our hands while he marched us (why did you always have to "march" when you were in trouble?) to the office and turned us into Coach Weatherby. That's when I learned about the razor strap.

We were, one at a time, still holding the butt of our cigarette, as per Coach Swift's orders, brought into Coach's office. When my turn came, I was admitted by Mrs. Fisher and, when the door closed, invited to sit down in a heavy oak chair. You could not miss seeing the razor strap that was hanging on a hook on the end of Coach Weatherby's desk.

I had to tell him what I had done like he had not already heard the same thing from all the boys who had gone in ahead of me. Then he explained the disciplinary process: "You have two choices," he started in. "You can either go home and tell your daddy (whom he knew very well) what you did. Then your daddy can write me a note and tell me that he has properly taken care of you. Or (here he paused and took a deep breath) I can give you a good whack across the knees with the razor strap and, if that is your choice, this will all remain between the two of us, and your daddy will not ever find out about it."

This was no choice at all. "Whip me now!" I blurted out. Nothing could have been worse than telling Daddy what had happened. I gladly sat up in the chair while Mr. Weatherby gave me one sharp whack across the knees with the razor strap. He then had me leave through the side door so that I could not give any clues to those still waiting about what was in store for them.

It was again in Mr. Swift's class when we were all sent to see Coach Weatherby later that same year. Mr. Swift could have a very bad temper with the boys' health and P.E. class. One day, his temper got out of control in the health classroom. I do not remember why, but we were all out of our seats and standing around when he came in the door. He turned red with anger and told us to, "Sit down ... sit down right now ... all of you sit down on the floor!" Lost in his anger, Mr. Swift had no idea that he had told us to sit down on the floor. We heard his blunder and decided to take it literally. So, we all sat down on the floor of the classroom instead of at our desks.

He called us "Impertinent and insubordinate," and herded us all to the office. This time, as we were individually taken into Coach Weatherby's private domain, we were not punished. Coach just told each of us that sometimes teachers got out of control and by doing it this way, Mr. Swift thought we had all been punished before being sent slowly back to class. I could not help but notice a little smile on his face as he talked with me.

It was not until my junior year that I had another disciplinary engagement with Mr. Weatherby. It was the spring of the year, and we had just had the "school is not out yet" speech at an assembly program. This year, his speech featured a whole chapter on squirt guns. Mr. Weatherby told us that there had been an epidemic of squirt guns on the campus and that they were not to be tolerated ... no more squirt guns!

Later that very afternoon, David Morgan and I were going up the outside stairs near the school office when we were hit by an unmistakable stream of squirt gun water. We rounded the brick column from which it came, and David and I caught Marvin Smith there.

Marvin was a mischievous boy who was smaller than either of us. David grabbed him around the chest, and I got his ankles. We carried him down to the office. We carried him straight past Mrs. Fisher's desk and into Mr. Weatherby's office, where we handed over the offending squirt gun and flopped Marvin right on top of the principal's desk.

Instead of giving us an award for good citizenship, Mr. Weatherby let Marvin go. Then he took David and me to the school library, where he made us look up and read aloud an encyclopedia article about vigilantes! We were offended!

After that time, I had no more face-to-face trouble with Coach Weatherby at school. He was still our respected Sunday School teacher at the Methodist Church, and about the only times I saw him up close were the Sunday morning class times.

Finally, our Senior year came at WTHS. My friends and

I had already been accepted to the colleges we were going off to the following year. The spring semester was almost a formality to end with graduation.

My best friend, David Morgan, was to be the valedictorian, and another of my good friends, Doug Robertson, was the salutatorian. I was in the top half-dozen of our graduating class of nearly two hundred and fifty. Coach Weatherby was exceedingly proud of our graduating class. It was the first class he could remember in which the valedictorian and salutatorian were boys. Besides that, there were several more of us right at the top of the class. He told us again and again how proud he was of this particular class.

We were well into the month of May when one day David, Doug, and I were together. We started talking about all the things we would never get to do again after we graduated from high school. After covering a few topics, David offered, "You know what? After we graduate, we will never have another chance to lay out of school. How can you skip school when you have already graduated? We better take advantage of these last weeks and lay out every chance we have." Doug and I agreed.

There was only one problem: David and I were both school bus drivers. (Yes, North Carolina had student bus drivers from the beginning of time until well after I had graduated.) How were we going to lay out of school and simultaneously deal with our school bus routes? Finally, we made a plan.

David and I would drive our bus routes as usual. Then when we got to school and our passengers were unloaded, we would walk around by the football stadium, where Doug would be waiting for us in the Jeep he was going to borrow from his older brother. Then we would be free for the day until we had to sneak back in the afternoon to drive our buses again. It was, to us, the perfect plan. It was brilliant. (How three boys at the top of their graduating class thought this was a brilliant plan remains an unanswered question.)

The big day arrived. I drove my morning school bus route. After the bus was empty, I didn't even make eye contact with David. We simply ignored each other as we walked unhurriedly around the end of the stadium. Back there was the Jeep with Doug waiting behind the wheel. He drove us away, and we waited until we were well out of sight before we hooted and congratulated each other on the free day unfolding ahead of us.

Our first plan was to drive up Big Stomp Mountain, where we had camped so many times at Mr. West's fox-hunting cabin. We did that. It only took us a couple of hours to go everywhere we wanted to go. Now what were we going to do next?

We were all hungry, so we decided we needed to go somewhere to get something to eat. The only problem was: where could we go? Everyone who worked at Charlie's Place and at Clyde's Restaurant knew all three of us. We couldn't dare go there. There was nowhere else in town to go. We would just have to be hungry for the rest of the day.

Even riding around was risky. Everyone knew us. At least they would not associate us with the Jeep. David and I slunk down low, and Doug tried to drive with his head down as we rode around. Finally, one of them had an idea. David and Doug both went to the Presbyterian Church, a church that was smaller than the Methodist Church where our family went. They both knew that there was nobody at their church during the day and that it was also always unlocked. So, we parked the Jeep on a side street and spent the rest of the day hiding in the Presbyterian Church's basement.

Several things happened during that day about which we did not know. As it was drawing close to graduation time, there was a rehearsal of some sort called by Coach Weatherby at school. That's when he discovered that three of the people involved in the graduation ceremony were not to be found. He discovered that we were all listed on the daily absentee report but that he had no requests for substitute bus drivers that day. He then discovered that David and I had indeed driven our buses that morning.

Mr. Weatherby had called my house, and, of course, no one answered. He also got no answer at Doug's house. When he called David's house and his grandmother answered the phone, she said, "Of course, he's not here ... he's at school."

The result of all this research was that when Doug dropped

David and me off behind the stadium, and we walked around the end to drive our buses that afternoon, Coach Weatherby was standing right there next to our buses waiting for us. We could both see that there were substitute drivers already sitting in the driver's seats, ready to take our routes for the afternoon.

He didn't even look at us. He just said, "Go into my office and wait for me, boys. I'll be there as soon as all the buses are gone."

The way the buses ran, it took some time for Coach Weatherby to finish with them. Besides the buses that originated from the high school bus lot, there were buses that came to us from elementary schools that did not arrive until some minutes after we got out of school. It seemed like we waited forever, worrying all the while until we heard the outer office door open. By now, Mrs. Fisher had gone home, so we knew it was Mr. Weatherby.

The second door opened, and he entered his office, where we were waiting. He didn't even look at us until he had walked around his desk and was seated in his big chair. He thought for a few minutes, and then he looked at us. "Where have you boys been?" David and I looked at the floor and did not volunteer an answer. "What have you been doing all day?" Neither of us said a thing. "Whose idea was this anyway?" By now, we were looking at our shoes with deep concentration.

Coach Weatherby stared out the window for a long moment. Then he looked at the two of us and asked, "What do you boys think I should do to you?"

I said nothing. David, however, was not to remain silent any longer. He, who grew up to become a Presbyterian minister, looked at Mr. Weatherby and then pointed at the razor strap. "I guess that's what I would do." He went on, "What I would do would be to take that razor strap and just flail the life out of us."

Mr. Weatherby's head went down on his desk. He just sat there like that for a few minutes, and then his head, still nestled in his arms, began to bounce on the desk. "He's laughing at us," David and I both thought. This was more frightening than ever.

Then Mr. Weatherby sat up, and we could see that he was not laughing. Tears were streaming down his face. He was crying as he moaned, "Oh Lord ... Oh Lord ... if this is what the best ones are doing, Oh Lord, what are the worst ones doing?"

He then told us that he had decided we did not deserve to get off with a whipping as it would be over in just a few minutes, and we needed punishment that would last longer. What we were going to have to do was stay in after school one day for each hour of school we had missed. He figured that would be seven days during which we would not be able to drive our buses. Seven days for which we would not get paid as bus drivers. Including this day, that would actually be the eighth day. We both breathed a sigh of relief. My biggest fear had been that I would have to tell my Daddy.

When we were finally set free to walk home, David came up with a bright idea. "Let's have a stay-in party," he said.

"What are you talking about?" I wanted to know.

"Think about it. It takes Coach most of an hour to get everyone dismissed and then to send off both rounds of buses after that. That means that he will not be around for probably the whole time we are supposed to stay in. So, let's call a few people and get them to bring Cokes and stuff to munch on, and they can stay in with us! We will have a party!" I thought the plan was excellent.

As soon as he heard about it, Bill McInvaille volunteered to bring a transistor radio. Several girls offered to supply snacks and drinks, and the plan was all set.

The next afternoon we reported to Mrs. Fisher in the office as soon as the last period bell sounded. "Where do we go?" one of us asked. She told us to just pick a room down the hall and to keep our own time. She said that our hour would most likely be over before Coach Weatherby even got back into the office. We could go home as soon as it was four-fifteen.

Our cohorts joined us, and we headed to the far end of the hall so our noise might not be heard back in the office. Out came the radio, and Bill tuned in WWIT in Canton, our preferred station. The drinks and snacks came out, and after a round of snacks, the dancing started.

He must have heard the noise coming from the room, because all of a sudden, with no warning at all, the door popped open.

There stood Coach Weatherby.

I can see the look on his face to this very day. It was a blend of anger, disappointment, and downright unbelief.

"What the ... is going on here?"

David answered, "We're staying in like you told us to. You didn't say we couldn't invite some company to be with us. After all, they might have done things they didn't get caught for ... and needed to stay in to be even."

Mr. Weatherby found his voice, "Get out of here ... all of you!" He turned to David and me. "You two, you two don't deserve to stay in. It's over! Get yourselves on home and start driving your buses again tomorrow." Then, to himself, he muttered, "Boy will I be glad when graduation is over!"

Well, we had gotten out of our punishment, but, the deadly worry of my Daddy finding out what we had done still kept me from sleeping at night.

The following Sunday, the lesson was on the Prodigal Son. In his remarks, Coach Weatherby reckoned that it was possible to disappoint your adults while you still were at home as much as going into a foreign country. It was a miserable lesson.

After church, we were at home, eating Sunday dinner

when Daddy spoke up. "You know, Lucille, I have to go to a District church meeting this evening. It's over in Canton at Central Methodist Church. Coach Weatherby and I are to represent our church. I'm going to pick him up, and we'll ride over there together."

I almost choked on my food. This was bad. It would take them about twenty minutes in the car each way, and there was no way that my father would return home innocent of my behavior. Even before he left that evening, I retreated to my room and pretended to do homework.

Daddy was only gone for a few hours, but it seemed like an eternity. I heard his car pulling the driveway hill, and my breathing became heavy. Maybe I could just faint and die before he got to me, which would save both of us a lot of trouble.

He called through the door of my room, "I stopped at Biltmore Dairy and got some ice cream on the way home. Come on in the kitchen ... I need to talk with you." My last meal was going to be Biltmore Dairy ice cream!

I slouched my way to the kitchen. Mama and my brother, Joe, were there already scooping out their servings. "Help yourself," my Mama smiled.

We all sat down and began to eat. Daddy started, "Well we had a good meeting. I needed to go because we were asking the District to contribute some funds for the cemetery project out at Crabtree. I was real interested in that.

"Coach Weatherby and I had an interesting talk on the way. Your name came up," he was looking at me. "We were talking about graduation, and you know what he said to me? He said, 'Joe, that boy of yours who is going off to college in the fall, that boy certainly is one fine young man.'" I almost collapsed in disbelief.

It was well over a decade later when I was visiting at home with my parents when my mother wanted to tell me something. "Do you know that Mr. Weatherby is in the hospital? He has serious congestive heart failure, and Mrs. Weatherby is scared for him. Why don't you go to see him?" There was no way out of a hospital visit. In fact, I wanted to see Coach if it might be my last chance.

I headed down to the new hospital, got his room number, and headed up the elevator. When I entered his room, he looked like he might be sleeping. But with the sound of the door opening, he looked immediately in my direction. "Donald Davis," he called my name before I had a chance to speak to him.

"Yes," I replied, "Mama told me you were here, and I wanted to come to see you." We proceeded to have a very fine visit. Time sometimes has the power to move painful events to the laughable past. Things were going so well that I brought up the incident of David, Doug, and me laying out of school before graduation. Mr. Weatherby's eyes brightened, and he laughed out loud. "I guess it was stuff like that that finally wore me out."

"What do you mean?"

"Oh, you know. The weight of carrying around all the things that parents just didn't need to know about their children. That's a heavy load sometimes, especially when it's good boys like you and David. At least Mary Emma and I shared a laugh about it when I told her that night. Eventually, you all made me proud that I had something to do with your growing up."

Coach Weatherby did not recover from that hospital stay. He died barely a week after that last visit. It is almost sad for me to realize what a good man he was, which I might never have learned if we had missed that last hour together.

Chapter Eleven

Keiffer Moody

KEIFFER MOODY WAS ONE OF MY FATHER'S COUSINS, my grand-mother Davis having been a Moody. I knew this to be true though my Mama would vehemently deny any connection between Keiffer and our family. He came from a good family. His father was both a successful politician and businessman. Being the youngest child in the family, he ended up inheriting a family home and enough assets that he was able to live comfortably without ever needing to hold down a job.

If, in the 1950s, you asked anyone in downtown Waynesville who Keiffer Moody was, they would unanimously reply that he was the town drunk.

It was said that Keiffer was proud of his position as the town drunk because he could afford to buy his own alcohol and was not beholden to others.

From my earliest memories, Keiffer was a fixture in downtown Waynesville. Whenever we went to town, Mama would be on the lookout for him. In the daytime, he was most likely to hang out around Felix Stovall's produce stand since you could buy beer there. The produce stand was beside a little alley that Keiffer cut through on his way to and from home. If he was not at Felix's, he might be found at Finney Timbes' Tavern on the other side of Main Street. Whenever we went up the street, Mama would be sure that we crossed over the street before we got to the produce stand just to be sure that we did not accidentally run into this scorned relative.

Since we never had direct contact with Keiffer, all my information about him came from hearsay and repeated stories. The canon of Keiffer stories was large, and its contents were repeated over and over again so that the stories gradually became known to everyone.

Just up the street from the produce stand and opposite the tavern was John Boyd's Furniture Store. In front of the furniture store, John had a line of rocking chairs, ostensibly for sale but also placed to be used by a club of men who were apt to hang out there throughout the afternoon. Beside the store door was one of those old weight-and-fortune scales that you step on, drop in your penny, and your fortune would come out in a little folded cardboard while your weight popped up on the face of the scale.

One day the men's club was holding their afternoon gathering when Keiffer came reeling down the street. He had been at the tavern for a while and seemed to be on his way home. As he approached, Keiffer pulled a penny out of his pocket and headed over toward where he knew the scales always lived. The problem that day was that the scales were out of whack. John had pulled them inside the store pending a service call. Keiffer stood there looking at a blank space and wondering why he could not find what he was looking for.

"What'chee looking for, Keiffer?" John asked while the other men watched.

Keiffer held up his penny, "I was wanting to weigh myself.... What happened to the scales?"

John smiled, "Oh, turn around, Keiffer. It's right behind you."

Keiffer turned around to face a parking meter that was, indeed, right behind him. He put his penny into the parking meter and gasped, "Oh, lord, I've lost a hundred pounds!" The stories were legion.

Finney Timbes often told the story of an evening when Keiffer had settled in at the tavern for a good while. It got to be on up after nine o'clock, and Finney was ready to close and go home. Everyone else was long gone, and Keiffer was the only one holding things up. Finally, Finney suggested, "Why don't we go home, Keiffer, I'm ready for some sleep." Keiffer looked all around the tavern like he had lost something.

"What are you looking, for, Keiffer? Aren't you about ready to go home?"

"I'm ready, Finney," he replied, "but I can't find my coat.

It's got to be cold out there."

Finney laughed, "You've already got it on, Keiffer. You haven't taken it off the whole time you've been here!"

"Oh, Finney," Keiffer shot back, "Thank you a million times for telling me that. Why, if you hadn't told me that, I would have plumb frozen to death on the way home!"

Through the years, Keiffer had made a number of appearances before Judge Howell in the courtroom, mostly for public drunkenness. (It was a good thing he never had a car or a driver's license.) After a while, Judge Howell got tired of seeing him there and worn out from having him spend one night in jail and then returning to his old habits the following day. Finally, at the end of one appearance, Keiffer was "sentenced" to a thirty-day commitment to the State Hospital down in Morganton.

A deputy was assigned to take Keiffer to Morganton the following day. There was only one car belonging to the Sheriff's Department. So, the plan was for the deputy to take Keiffer down on the Trailways bus. Then the deputy could ride back to Waynesville after he had turned Keiffer in.

Handcuffed to Keiffer, the deputy got on the bus for the bus trip. In those days the bus to Morganton stopped in every little town. The stop-and-go trip could take a couple of hours.

Before the bus was on the other side of Asheville, the deputy had fallen sound asleep. There he was, sleeping right beside Keiffer, to whom he was handcuffed but with the big ring of keys visible and in easy reach. When he didn't wake up through the stop at Oteen, Keiffer lifted the keys, unlocked himself, relocked the deputy to the armrest on the bus seat, and got off at the next stop at Swannanoa. He hitchhiked back home long before the deputy got loose and returned by Trailways.

One day my brother, Joe, and I were in town with Mama. We were walking up the street so she could go to Sadie Hale's Dress Shop when, without time to escape, Keiffer popped out of the little alley beside the produce stand. There we were, face to face! "Lucille Davis!" he exclaimed. "Well, it is nice to see you!" Then he looked at me and Joe, saying, "I'm glad we ran into each other. Do your boys know what an important man I am in this town?"

All Mama could do was look disgusted. She didn't need to answer. Keiffer had a speech to make, and he was going to make it. "Lucille Davis, I am an important man in this town because it is people like me who give people like *you* a gift. The gift I give to you is that, because of me, you get to live with the belief that you don't have anything wrong with you!" Then he took a bow, and we were gone.

That night at the supper table, she had to tell Daddy what had happened. "That man," she wouldn't even say his name, "he is so awful. He is just so dumb and terrible."

Daddy just waited a minute for her to simmer down.

"Lucille, don't be so hard on Keiffer. First of all, he is not dumb. Back in school, he was one of the smartest kids with math that you've ever seen. He just took the wrong road too many times, and now he can't find his way back to the highway. Just let him go!" I didn't understand his metaphors, but I knew he was defending his old cousin.

There was one time when Keiffer came to church. We were all there, as usual, and the service was just about to begin when Keiffer stepped loudly into the back door of the sanctuary. He just stood there, and everyone seemed to turn and stare at him. All of a sudden, Keiffer had a sneezing fit. He sneezed and sneezed for what seemed to be three or four minutes. Then he stopped and said out loud, "Guess I must be allergic to this place," and walked back out the door.

On a later occasion, Keiffer found himself once again in front of Judge Howell. This time, with the sheriff present, Keiffer was sentenced to a lengthy commitment at the State Hospital in Morganton. Not wanting to be embarrassed again, the sheriff agreed to drive Keiffer down to Morganton himself and personally check him in. All went well this time, and the commitment was made.

About a week later, one of Keiffer's cousins decided he would drive down for a visit. The cousin was checked in at the visitors' desk, identified himself with his driver's license, and was shown the way back to see Keiffer.

They visited for a while, and then the cousin asked Keiffer

if he needed anything while he was there. Keiffer quickly replied, "There's a little canteen they have down the hall here for the 'inmates' like me. You can get chewing gum and candy and cigarettes there. If you'll loan me your billfold for a couple of minutes, I might like to get something there before you head back home." The billfold was handed over.

Keiffer took the billfold, which contained his cousin's driver's license, and headed straight to the check-in security desk. He approached the security guard who was handling the visitation process.

"I've been back there visiting my cousin, Keiffer Moody, he announced. He is in bad shape. He doesn't know much of anything. I think, half the time, he is even mixed up about who he is. I've had about all the visiting with him I can take!" The security guard marked him off the list, and Keiffer, billfold in hand, walked out the door of the State Hospital.

With his cousin's billfold, he could afford to get a taxi to the bus station and buy a bus ticket back to Waynesville. Without his billfold, the cousin spent a long day in the State Hospital before he finally convinced the staff that they had been hoodwinked, and he was released.

The Keiffer stories grew and grew. When you thought you had heard them all, someone would come up with another occasion on which this brilliant man had left his impact on the world.

It was told that one day Keiffer was crossing the street at the East Street traffic light when the first car in line at the red light was a Cadillac with Florida license plates. The two well-dressed women in the Cadillac had rolled their windows all down in the comfortable summer weather.

As Keiffer reeled across the street in front of them, one of the women was heard to say to the other, "There certainly are some strange, weird people in this little town!"

Keiffer, hearing this, made his way over to the open window on the driver's side of the car. He leaned down on the windowsill and announced to them, "Yes, ma'am. But most of you will go back to Florida after Labor Day!"

I was a very socially-awkward child during my high school years. I never had a girlfriend and was extremely shy on most group occasions. There was, however, one thing that I hoped for—membership in a group called the Tally-Ho Club at our high school. Everyone whom I thought to be anyone was a member of the Tally-Ho Club. More than any social goal, I wanted to be asked to join this club where I would mix with the in-crowd of my age group.

Sure, enough, after my freshman year, the invitation came. I received an official invitation to become a member of the Tally-Ho Club.

The bid came at the end of the school year, and my inclusion would start at the opening of the new school year in

September. However, there was mention that an initiation event of some type would occur as soon as school started. I figured this would be some joining ritual that all the new members would need to go through before confirmation as full Tally-Ho'ers.

The initiation event was announced for a Saturday night just after school started. It was to be held on the steps of the county courthouse just off Main Street in Waynesville.

Waynesville was very much a tourist town even in those days. Many people, mostly from Florida, spent whole summers there. Main Street was a lively place through the summer, and in September, it was still a busy place since many people did not go back South until after the leaves changed in October.

The two auction houses on Main Street were the centers of evening activity in the summer. Auctioneers held loud estate auctions. Many people who had no intention of buying anything still hung out at the auction houses for entertainment. Main Street was a busy place.

We gathered on the front steps of the courthouse, and the ritual started. Newly-invited members received assignments, most of which were designed to be embarrassing, and everyone, *except the one being initiated,* laughed and laughed. Some people who had no talent were required to make up songs about embarrassing topics *and sing them.* Dancing was expected from some who were profoundly uncoordinated. I watched the proceedings wondering what I would have to do when my name was called. Time—and the repeated process—proceeded at a snail's pace.

Suddenly, I was the only one left who had not been through the initiation process. Then I heard my name called.

As I walked up to the Court House steps, an older girl met me and handed me something. "This is mine ... but I think it will fit you just right!" I looked down and saw that she had handed me a yellow, one-piece girl's bathing suit. "Go inside to the restroom and put this on ... here's the cap to go with it ... and when you come back out, we will tell you what you have to do."

My face felt hot with embarrassment, but I did so want to be socially accepted by this group that I, indeed, went inside the courthouse and put on the bathing suit. It was very tight on me as the girl from whom it came was tiny. Returning to the crowd, I was greeted by roars of laughter ... and I had not even been told what I had to do yet.

"Now," the announcer instructed, "here is what you are going to do." She handed me a plumber's friend that had four rolls of toilet paper threaded onto the plunger handle. Then she handed me a necklace made out of ten full rolls of toilet paper strung together. She looped the necklace over my head as people roared in laughter.

"This is your assignment," she continued. "You need to go up and down Main Street and auction off all of those rolls of toilet paper. You need to get a dollar for each roll. You will come back without the toilet paper but with fourteen dollars. We will stay here and wait out of sight until you get back. Have fun!"

There was no choice. I had to either endure the embarrassment of actually doing as I had been instructed or undertake the even greater embarrassment of withdrawing from the Tally-Ho Club in front of all of the people whom I wanted most to impress. I took off and headed toward Main Street.

The courthouse was set back from Main Street, and as soon as I got out to the street itself, I had to cross over Depot Street to head up Main to where all the people would be. Right there on the corner was the bank building where my Daddy worked. I knew where I was but had no idea what I was doing. Once I crossed Depot Street, the Tally-Ho members back at the Court House were out of sight. They didn't want to be associated with what they asked me to do. They just wanted to laugh about it

I was walking in front of the bank building. Just beyond was the narrow parking lot where Daddy and the other bank employees parked during the workday. It was almost a dark alley. I was about to pass in front of that little alley when, all of a sudden, someone called out to me.

"Little Davis!" The voice was Keiffer Moody's. He was in the process of cutting through the little parking alley, and he saw me as I was slinking up Main Street. "Come here. Why in all of God's creation are you looking like this?" Keiffer did not laugh. In fact, he looked very sympathetic. "Sit down over here on this wall. Tell me what has got into you."

I sat down with him on the wall, just back off the street in the partial darkness, and I cried while I told him everything that was happening and what I was supposed to be doing. Keiffer just shook his head.

"Lord, lord," he muttered.

"Son," he didn't seem drunk at all right now, "I don't even go to church, but I sure know better than to treat somebody the way you are being treated. Making fun of another person is never something to laugh about."

Then Keiffer said, "Give me that wiping paper ... give me all of it." He took the plumber's friend and my necklace. Then threw all fourteen rolls of toilet paper in a trash barrel in the parking alley. Then he took out his billfold. "I'm not going to give you a ten-dollar bill, no. If I did that, they would know you didn't sell it as you were supposed to." He then counted out fourteen one-dollar bills, some of which were worn thin and dirty. He handed them to me.

"Don't go back over there right now ... They will know that you haven't had long enough to do the whole job. Let's just sit here and talk a little while. Then you can go back."

And that is exactly what we did.

I would like to say that I decided not to be a member of the Tally-Ho Club, but, I was neither mature enough nor wise enough to make that decision. I wanted too much to be included. But, that night, I was also initiated into another club—the Appreciation and Understanding of Keiffer Moody Club.

I think, for that one act for a fifteen-year-old boy, Keiffer, the man, deserves to be remembered.

Chapter Twelve

Jim and Roy

THIS IS THE STORY OF A GREAT ADVENTURE I had with two of my former teachers. I was eighteen years old. Jim Crocker was thirty-three years old. Roy Haupt was forty-eight years old. My father was sixty-three years old. I realized, through hindsight, that there was exactly a fifteen-year age gap between each two of the four of us.

Roy Haupt was my first male teacher. Until the eighth grade, the only men we ever saw in school were either running the place or not doing much of anything—the janitor and the principal. This year was to be different. This year, we were to be divided into "college preparatory" and "vocational education." In the college preparatory track, there were four teachers.

"I hope you get Roy Haupt," my Mama had said before school started. I was not listening to her at all as I had no control over who my teacher might be.

But when my cousin, Kay, said, "You will want to be in

Mr. Haupt's room. He is the best," I began to hope for that choice as well.

Sure enough, on that first day of school, I was assigned to Roy Haupt for the eighth grade. (We did not yet change classes in the eighth grade, so, Mr. Haupt would be my teacher for everything except band and art, including physical education.)

Our first view of Roy Haupt was of his back. He was writing his name on the board as we entered the room. Once finished, he turned around and said to us. "I am Roy Haupt, your teacher. I am the only man who ever served in the United States Army who could smoke a cigarette in the shower without it going out!" This was his way of telling us that he knew he had the biggest, longest nose we had ever seen, and he was going to make the first joke before we had a chance to laugh at it. From then on, he was always at least one step ahead of us.

On that first day of school, he told us that we were going to spend the year studying art. When some of the boys moaned, he countered, "Don't you know what art really is? Art is what happens when you do something; it could be anything, if done right, that takes your mind to a place where your body cannot go right now. If I can't make it art, it is not worth teaching!"

And that is what he did. From math to history to science, every day, we traveled out of our bodies into our minds. No one minded going to school with this genius of a man for a teacher.

He taught us to play bridge. He taught us to play chess.

He brought old wooden tennis rackets, and, instead of soft-ball, we played tennis during PE. We learned to read every kind of map he could find: road maps, topographical maps of the mountains where we lived, weather maps, large and small-scale maps of the countries of the world. We created imaginary brokerage accounts and, each morning read the Stock Market report in the *Asheville Citizen* and then made our imaginary trades for the day. We kept imaginary bank accounts and learned to fill out tax returns.

"Boys and girls," he addressed us, "The eighth grade is your last chance to learn everything you need to know about life. Next year, you will be in high school, and, unfortunately, in high school, you will have mostly courses instead of teachers. I may be your last actual teacher!"

At the end of our first day, Mr. Haupt explained to us, "Boys and girls. We sure have talked a lot today. But, do you know, that out of all the talking we do each day, there are ac-tually only four things that you need to remember forever.... The big question is: which four?" Then he explained to us that during the last twenty minutes of each day, three of us will be called on to present the four things from that day that we, individually, think are the ones to be remembered. Then, until the bell rings, we, as a class, get to argue about those things. We loved it. You never knew who was going to be called on until the end of the day, so all day, you were on the lookout for your choice of four things.

We did not know that he was discovering what we had learned that day versus what we had missed and allowing us to reinforce everything he had tried to teach us during that day. It was brilliant!

The best thing, to me, about Mr. Haupt was his love of geology. We lived in the extremely mineral-rich North Carolina mountains, and Mr. Haupt was a devoted rock collector. He had started his life planning to go to the Colorado School of Mines and major in geology, but World War II came along, as did marriage, and he finished as an Education major at the University of Miami. Still, rock collecting was his passion.

He infected many of us with his hobby. I began to seriously expand my rudimentary rock collection.

Sometimes on a Saturday, Mr. Haupt took some of us on rock-collecting trips. In his red Jeep CJ, he could fit four in the back, riding on the shelves over the wheel wells, and a fifth in the front. We would go to places like Copper Hill, Tennessee, and even up to Spruce Pine and the North Carolina Mineral Museum.

Because of my serious interest in rock collecting, Mr. Haupt was not finished with me when that eighth-grade year was over. I continued to visit him at home, and he continued to invite me along to rock and mineral shows in Asheville and on collecting trips. We moved from a teacher-student relationship to being permanent friends.

Jim Crocker arrived as our new band director at the outset of my tenth-grade year.

The Waynesville High School band was founded in 1941 by Charles Isley, and in 1950, Robert Campbell (his story is also in this collection) was added as junior high director and assistant high school director. The music program had grown, and the band, from the beginning of competitions, had received the highest grades in both marching and concert seasons.

Then the unthinkable happened. Mr. Campbell left for California in 1958, and the following year Mr. Isley departed to head the music department at Appalachian State University. The whole town was devastated.

No one would have been able to successfully carry the program forward without some backslide, and it was very unfortunate that the following two years saw the band get its first less-than-superior rating ever. Mr. Isley's not-to-be-named-here successor was hardly to blame; there was simply too much to live up to.

In addition to the second level rating in marching band competition at the Southeastern Marching Band Competition in Bristol, Tennessee, that next year a band member got sick at the outdoor October competition event and died shortly after returning home. Things were at a low ebb. The director left to take a college job, and we were in the market once again for a new leader.

That's when Jim Crocker was hired. He was thirty-one years old and had just married during the summer before coming to Waynesville. He arrived driving a baby-blue 1959 Ford retractable hardtop convertible with his beautiful new wife, Leigh. The whole town was enthralled, but the pressure was on.

Mr. Campbell had now been gone for three years, and his successor had not been successful in giving the seventh and eighth graders the kind of start that equipped them for high school musicianship. Jim Crocker was in a hole without a shovel. The only way to go was up.

Mr. Crocker immediately won the hearts of band members and parents alike. In no time, we were putting together half-time shows that made the community proud again. Then it was time for the Southeastern Marching Band Competition. This would be the test for our new director: could we recover the superior rating that had evaded us in the competition last year? We all worked diligently.

The competition weekend came just after football season was over. It was cold November. We left Waynesville on our chartered buses at five in the morning to cross the mountain to Tennessee in time to stop for breakfast. By ten a.m., we were in line for the giant parade of bands.

Bands from all over the Southeast were there. They were classed in grades one through six, depending on the size of the high school from which they came. In the parade, we went in order, from the ones through the sixes, down State Street in Bristol, the center line of which is the Tennessee-Virginia state boundary. We were a grade six band because we were in the largest size category. We always came next to the end alphabetically, with only Wytheville, Virginia, coming after Waynesville.

Competitions started in the afternoon. It was bitterly cold, and Mr. Crocker had us stay inside the school rather than sit out in the stadium. Everyone remembered the unfortunate death following the competition the year before. Bands competed in the same order as marching in the parade, alphabetically in categories one through six. Our turn on the field did not come until nearly midnight.

As dusk became night, a cold rain began to fall—first slowly and lightly, then increasing. With no alternate plan, bands continued to take the field in the increasing downpour. The organizers offered no alternative. We dressed and prepared mentally to go out and do our best.

Mr. Crocker was nowhere to be seen. Charlie Hipps, our drum major, pulled everyone together and gave us a little pep talk. I heard, "Our moment…" and "Can't disappoint Mr. Crocker." About when his speech ended, Mr. Crocker came back into the room where we were suiting up.

"You probably wondered where I have been. Well, let me tell you. I have been on the phone with Mr. Weatherby and Mr. Leatherwood." We, of course, knew them to be our principal and our school superintendent. "I called them about the weather. Do you all remember what happened when a student got sick last year? Well, let me tell you, your health is much more important than every trophy in the world. So, with the advice and agreement of both Mr. Weatherby and Mr. Leatherwood, we are not going to go out onto the field in this freezing rain. We are going to go back to our rooms and get a warm night of sleep and head back home in the morning with every one of you alive and well."

With this decision, Mr. Crocker won the hearts of every band parent at Waynesville High School. He had dared make a difficult decision for the good of us all. The next day our buses were met at the Haywood County line by a motorcade of cheering parents and supporters. With streamers flying and horns blowing, they paraded behind our buses back to the high school, cheering us for our work and celebrating our health and safety.

The following year we returned to the Marching Band Contest and regained our number one Superior rating. In the years to come, Jim Crocker's Waynesville Township High School and later Tuscola High School (the successor school when the county reorganized the overall system) achieved the highest ratings ever given at the Bristol contest.

Mr. Crocker and I became great friends. We played together in a little local band led by music store owner Hal Strain. It was called "Strains of Music." Even into my adulthood, Mr.

Crocker and I remained in touch with admiration, respect, and appreciation.

When Mr. Crocker was just past seventy, and with awareness of his health difficulties, former band members decided to hold an appreciation banquet honoring him for his years of teaching and positive influence on students. Notices sent out for reservations garnered so many responses that there was no place in or around Waynesville big enough to hold the event. It was finally planned for a large center on the Western Carolina University campus. When notified that it was happening, Jim Crocker asked that I be invited to emcee the event.

We had a great time with more than five hundred former band members in attendance. We included sixteen former students who were making their living as professional musicians. They formed a swing band that provided music for the banquet evening. After the meal, there were many speeches filled with fun, tears, and laughter.

At the end of the evening, Jim and I reminisced about his first years in Waynesville. That first year, when we were rained out of the Marching Band Contest, came up. When I mentioned it, Jim laughed. "That rain saved my tail," he started. "I did not know what bad shape the band program had fallen into when I took the job. I was still thinking I was inheriting Charlie Isley's band. Not so. We were in bad shape. We were all working hard, especially all of you students. We were in no way ready to compete for a top award. It was going to be embarrassing, and I was going to go down in history as the person who failed to restore the program to its deserved glory. When that cold rain started falling, and I remembered the tragic death the year before, I could feel salvation on the way! When I made that phone call and told Mr. Weatherby and Mr. Leatherwood what I was going to do, they were in total agreement, and I breathed a big sigh of relief. We had gotten a reprieve! I was energized for the coming year, and that gave us time to get things together. That rain saved my life and my job!

"My contract might not have been renewed if we had marched and made another non-superior award. I've never told anyone this before except Leigh. Now you know the whole story."

Less than a year after that, Jim and Leigh both died in the same year.

Sometime back in high school, I discovered that Roy Haupt and Jim Crocker had become best friends. It may have had to do with a mutual appreciation of Scotch whisky, but, more than that, they shared very similar human values.

Early during my senior year, I was accepted to go to Davidson College the following year. My dad was in his sixties and was not a very active parent. We had more of a grandparent-to-grandchild relationship. My mother was worried about my going off to college and she kept bugging me to "talk with my Daddy" before I left home. I could not figure out what she wanted me to "talk" about. What I did not know was that she had also bugged both Roy Haupt and Jim Crocker to "talk with Donald before he goes off to college."

So ... one day, shortly after graduation, I was at Roy Haupt's house where we were looking at some of his mineral collection and a new set of cabinets he had built for display. The phone rang. Roy answered the phone and whispered to me that he was talking with Jim Crocker.

"Yeah," he said into the phone. "His mother's been trying to get me to 'talk to him' before he goes off to college. Wants me to give him a lot of advice to get him ready to be away from home." Then there was a long moment of silence as Jim was pushing his side of the conversation. Roy smiled at me. "That's a great idea. I'll ask him about it and then you can ask his mother if it will be okay with her." They talked a little bit more and then he hung up the phone.

"That was Jim Crocker. He and I have been planning to go on a little rock-hunting trip for about a week starting this Sunday. Do you know that your mother has been bugging both of us to tell you a few things about life before you go off to college? She doesn't think your dad will do that since he never had the kind of chance that you are going to have. Jim suggested that we just take you on the trip with us and we would have plenty of chances to visit and talk along the way. We will be gone for a week. How about it?"

How about it? I thought. I would rather do nothing more than this. There was one more full week before my summer job at the bookstore started, and this would fill the time perfectly.

"Jim is going to call your mother and ask her about it. You don't need to tell her that this is already in the plan ... she will just think he had a spontaneous idea. I bet she will go along with it." I knew she would.

Mr. Crocker must have called her as soon as he and Roy hung up because when I got home in less than an hour, he had already called. Mother was thrilled that I was going to have this week of personal tutoring from two of my favorite teachers. She knew they were the ones to prepare me properly to go away from home. As supper that night, my Daddy added his agreement. The next day I packed my duffle and began the three long days until our Saturday departure.

We planned to take Jim's Ford convertible. Since the hard top went down into the trunk space, there was very little luggage room. We were limited to one bag each—whatever might fit in the half of the back seat where I was not riding. That was all we needed.

It was early on Saturday morning when the blue Ford came up the driveway to our house. Both Daddy and Mama went out to greet Jim and Roy. My parents had both insisted that I call them "Mr. Crocker and Mr. Haupt," though I had already been calling them "Jim" and "Roy" since graduation.

We all visited a little bit. Roy promised Mama that I would call a couple of times during the week if there was a way to do so but not to worry if that didn't work out. Daddy swung my duffle bag into the car, and we were on our way.

Jim had deliberately left the convertible top up when they picked me up. He was aware that we didn't want Mama to think this was going to be a carefree trip! As far as she was concerned, it was a science field trip where we were studying the geology of rocks and minerals in North Carolina. Before we were a mile from the house, he pulled over to the side of the highway and we put the top down. It would stay down for the sunny days during the trip.

Before coming to be the band director in Waynesville, Jim Crocker had been the band director in Hamlet, North Carolina, a small-town east of Charlotte in the vicinity of the former gold mining region of the state. There would be lots of old mine tailings for us to explore. Another reason for going there, though, was that Jim had old friends who owned a small cabin on a little lake called "Ledbetter's Pond" outside of Hamlet.

We drove most of the day to get there. We went by the house where Jim's friends lived, met them, and got the key. Then it was off to the cabin.

Ledbetter's Pond was an old mill pond that had been built to create power for a former textile mill that was built there. It was not large, mostly a place for recreation and fishing.

What had been called a "cabin" was just a small wooden house right on the edge of the water. It had three small bedrooms, and so we each claimed a room of our own. There was a kitchen, but we had no plans for cooking. No, there were other plans for eating.

Straight across on the opposite side of the lake, there was a private restaurant that belonged to one of the men's civic clubs in town. It might have been something like the Elks Club or another such organization. In those days, North Carolina was a dry state as far as bars or restaurants were concerned. The few exceptions included "the private club." This meant that clubs, like country clubs or other clubs that only admitted members, could have bars, or serve drinks with meals. Jim told us all about this and that this was his plan for our supper that night.

"Are you a member?" Roy asked. "If it is for members only, how will we be able to eat there?"

Jim laughed, "You don't have to be real members," he said. "When we get to the door, they will charge us a dollar each and have us fill out a membership card. Then we will be 'members' for the next week."

We all laughed about that. Then we heard the next part of the plan.

"You might have noticed that there is a little outboard motorboat out by the dock." Roy and I had noticed. When we had picked up the key, the owners had told us that the boat had plenty of gas and we were free to use it all we wanted. "I thought," he went on, "That we could take the boat over to supper. That way, if we happen to have something to drink, we won't be driving back when we shouldn't." We all laughed some more.

All of my mountain ancestors had been dedicated Methodists ever since the Methodist Church was established in 1784. In those days, the Methodist Church was very strict about alcohol. Both my parents had also grown up in the moonshining rural parts of Haywood County and were opposed to the very existence of alcoholic beverages. Now my two favorite teachers were taking me to a place where alcohol was not only served, but they were talking about *actually drinking* some! I was excited.

We got ready to go and jumped in the little boat. It was about twenty feet long with a ten-horsepower engine. Jim pulled the cord, and the motor started right up.

The three of us made the boat sit pretty low in the water as we moved slowly across the lake. Roy and I did not know about the other reason we were moving slowly. Suddenly the boat bumped against something hidden below the surface of the dark water. We looked at Jim.

"Oh, that," he started, "When they built the pond, nobody thought about clearing the trees from the land that was going to be under the water. They filled up the pond, and a lot of the trees stuck up out of the water. What they did was to just go out in a boat with a chainsaw and cut the trees off as close as they could to the water line. Through the years, the tops of the stumps have rotted off until they are out of sight below the water, but they are still right down there. We have to go slowly, but it won't be dangerous." Okay, I thought, he is an adult, and I should trust him. I was meeting two different people from the teacher-personas through which I had always known these two men.

We landed at the club/restaurant dock. There were several other boats tied up there just like ours was. This seemed to be a normal way to go to supper for people who lived on the pond. Once at the door, we each paid our own dollar, filled out our membership card, and we were "members."

Inside the building, it was like a very nice restaurant. All the people eating there were well-dressed and nice-looking. We were seated, and menus were delivered.

Across the back of the room was the first bar I had ever seen in my life. There were fascinating and decorative bottles of every shape and color on tiered, mirrored shelves behind the busy barkeeper. I couldn't take my eyes away.

Before the waitress returned to our table, Roy turned to me and said, "Your mother wanted me and Jim to talk to you before you went off to college. So, we are going to talk. To-night, we are going to talk about alcohol. Here is the first thing you need to learn: don't drink cheap beer!"

When the waitress came, Jim spoke up immediately, "We will have three Heinekens, please."

The woman looked at me and asked, "Are you eighteen?" (This was the legal drinking age in those days.) I pulled out my driver's license, and she saw that I had been eighteen for all of six days!

The first taste was bitter to me, but when the steaks came, it all went together deliciously. Roy and Jim had a second one, but they decided that one was best for me on this first night.

We finished our dinner and headed back down to the boat dock. It was dark by now, and we talked about how it was fortunate that we had left some lights on at the house across the little lake. Ours was the only illuminated cabin in that vicinity, so it would be easy to find. The boat had no lights of any kind; we putted across in the dark.

We must have hit ten of the underwater stumps on our way back. I was assigned the front of the boat as the lookout, but since the night and the water were both dark, I never managed to see anything in time to keep us from hitting it. It was bump, bump, bump, but we made it back safely.

We settled down for the night ... I thought. I went to bed and was in the process of falling asleep when I heard Roy and Jim talking and laughing. They were discussing two new books that they had both recently read. It sounded interesting to me, so instead of going to sleep, I sat up in bed and began to listen closely.

The two books were both by a man named Alfred Kinsey, though Roy said he had help from other researchers. They were both scientific studies, and I was very interested in science. One of the books was called *Sexual Behavior in the Human Male,* and the other one, the more interesting one, was called *Sexual Behavior in the Human Female.*

I must have listened for much more than an hour while I learned *behaviors* I had never thought of even asking about. (My parents were as open about sex as they were about alcohol.) My mother wanted these two teachers to "talk to me," but I was getting more than she bargained for! It was great.

The following day we had a great rock-hunting adventure. We were about an hour to the old Reed Gold mine back toward Charlotte. This was where the largest single gold nugget ever found in the United States was found back before the California gold discovery. We found some decent crystallized quartz pieces and some iron pyrite nearby. We then drove up to a little place called Gold Hill.

Roy asked some men in a little store about where we could find some old gold mine sites, and they directed us to find where a man called "Pappy Hayes" lived. They told us he lived right beside an old mine and that he was always interested in stuff like that.

We easily found the house, but no one was at home. It was an old two-story house with porches both downstairs and upstairs. The house had not been painted for decades, and it looked to be on the verge of falling down. The upstairs porch was fenced with chicken wire, and a passel of dogs barked at us from there. Mineral samples almost filled the old front porch, so we knew the old-timer was a rockhound, indeed.

Since the old man was not at home, we did look around a little bit to see if we could find where the old gold mine had been. The yard was overgrown, but scattered through the weeds and high grass, there were a half-dozen old, broken-down Packard ambulances and hearses. If they were restored, it could be quite a collection.

We did see where an old mine shaft was now covered up, but we made no real discoveries there. Still, just visiting that old house was worth the trip.

That night was a repeat of the night before but with accelerated education for me. We crossed the pond in the little boat and showed our membership cards at the door. Once inside and seated, my education about alcohol continued. "Tonight, you are ready to learn about mixed drinks," Roy started. He and Jim were both having gin and tonics, but they decided that the best place for me to begin was with a whisky sour.

I liked the whisky sour. Now I know that the bartender probably realized what they were doing and had gone light on the bourbon and heavy on the simple syrup for me.

When dinner was eaten, I thought we were ready to go

home. No. My good teachers told me that I now needed to learn about "after-dinner cordials."

They ordered several in tiny glasses so that I could taste them all. Some were a little bit strong for me, but I did like the one called "Baileys."

When we got back that night, my teachers invited me to stay up and join in the book discussion. I did, but, after my "night of drinking," I voluntarily soon headed to bed.

We stayed at the cabin one more day, during which we drove over near Albemarle to the Stanley County Pyrophyllite Company. This was a great stop. I selected some beautiful samples of crystalline pyrophyllite with greenish circular patterns.

That final night we again ate at the "club." I was to make all my own choices on this night. I started cautiously with a small filet and another Heineken. I expressed no preference for an after-dinner drink.

As we traveled east after finding the Pyrophyllite in Stanly County, there were no more good mineral stops in Eastern North Carolina. The mountains of our western counties are our most mineral-laden part of the state. There was only one place Roy still wanted to visit at our far-east destination. It was the Aurora Fossil Beds outside the little town of Aurora, east of Washington, North Carolina.

We drove to Greenville, where we visited East Carolina University. Jim told us that Bobby Buckner, one of my best band buddies, might be interested in going to school there.

We found a motel in Greenville where we requested an extra roll-away—for me—and cheaply spent the night there. The following day, we started out early and got to Aurora.

There was a phosphate mine on the banks of the Pungo River where the tailings of the mining operation contained many fossilized shark teeth and other fossils from the Miocene Period. We did find a place to have lunch in the tiny town, and people we met told us that they were trying to get the state to build a museum there. They thought this might attract tourists and help the town economically. Glad we had the place to ourselves, we dug up several good and quite large shark-tooth fossils.

After one last night in Greenville, we headed back on our way to Waynesville. It would take us two days to get home since Roy was determined that we had to go by Spruce Mine on the Blue Ridge Parkway and visit the North Carolina Minerals Museum.

The museum was my favorite rock-collecting part of the whole trip. The museum was filled with beautiful specimens of minerals ranging from aquamarine beryl crystals to emeralds and all kinds of quartz crystals. They were beyond my collecting imagination.

Then, it was our final day, and we headed for home. By now Jim and Roy had truly "talked to me" about everything. We had covered all the vices first and kept on talking about them for part of each day. But I also soaked up their good advice about academic habits and study wisdom as well.

Roy's advice to me was to try to buy my textbooks as soon as I got to campus for orientation. Then he said I should write out by hand my own copy of the contents of each textbook and memorize that table of contents. It would then be my own organizational outline for the course.

He also told me that I should read the first couple of chapters of each text before the first lecture class met. That way, I would have a head start on understanding what the professor was talking about. He said that if I actually outlined what I read ahead of time, I might not even have to take notes about everything, and I could listen a lot better.

The other trick I should learn was to ask a lot of questions, whether smart or dumb. He said you got a lot of credit for just acting interested!

Jim's main advice was to be sure that I kept up some time for play—just music—real play.

Though they were at least a decade ahead of my timeline, they also gave me one bit of advice about marriage that I remember to this day. Again, it was Jim Crocker who voiced it: "Son ... if you want to be happy for a year, marry a body. If you want to be happy for the rest of your life, marry a personality! You will forget this advice when you first need it, but it will come back to you later." He turned out to be right about everything he said.

All this advice was good, but the most important thing

was that it gave me something I could tell Mama about what we had "talked about" on our trip to distract her from needing to know anything about sex and alcohol (and a few other interesting forbidden topics!).

It was late afternoon when we put the top up on the blue convertible and turned up the driveway hill at my house. Mama was standing and looking out the window, waiting for our arrival. (She might have been standing there all week for all I knew!)

She met us at the car, and Daddy also came. She invited the now-renamed Mr. Haupt and Mr. Crocker to have supper with us, but they also wanted to just get home. And so, we said goodbye at the end of a week that all three of us had enjoyed greatly.

For much more than the rest of the summer, I remembered that trip. For much more than my entire college career, I remembered that trip. In fact, for all of the rest of my life, I have sincerely and thankfully remembered that trip and the two great men who "talked to me!"

Roy Haupt died of a heart attack at age sixty-three. He had smoked too many of those cigarettes in the shower in the Army and beyond. He never retired from teaching; no, he just quit when he was about sixty. He told me that they were trying to get him to "just stick to the book" and stop "all that foolishness about maps and chess and stock market accounts." He told me that he chose to quit teaching rather than lower his standards. I thank him for who he was.

Chapter Thirteen

Miss Stella

WHEN ODYSSEUS WENT OFF TO THE TROJAN WAR, he left his wife, Penelope, and his son, Telemachus, behind at home. He also asked one of his old friends, Mentor, to be the person to look out for Telemachus while he was gone. This was Mentor's task, and this caretaking role became the origin of our word "mentor."

Note one important thing at this point: Telemachus did not choose Mentor.

The secret, however, was that it was not, in fact, Mentor who was giving guidance and care to Telemachus. No, whenever Mentor appeared to have any contact with Telemachus, it was Athena, the Goddess of Wisdom, who disguised herself as Mentor so that he never knew he was being cared for and guided by the goddess herself. The Goddess was the one who chose him, he did not choose her, and he did not know of her care for him until much later.

This is the true, literal meaning of the word "mentor." A real mentor is not someone we choose; it is instead someone who chooses us. In addition, the choice is not announced, it is done in secret. This is because when we are getting the real guidance that we need, we are not smart enough to accept and follow it unless it is somehow wound around us by one of greater wisdom so that we do not know enough about what is happening to avoid it. What a life-blessing it is to have such a mentor!

This story is the story of a mentor in my life. It was my good fortune to discover the wholeness of the story years after the events themselves; I might have lived my life without ever gaining the appreciation that came with the revelation of the truth.

My Daddy's family settled on a homesteading farm in the north end of Haywood County. The first family land of ours in that part of the world goes back as early as 1781 and the first presence of organized religion in the same territory came with the Methodist circuit riders who traveled through on their circuit as early as 1784. So, by default as much as by choice, our family became early Methodists.

To get to town from that farm, they took the dirt country road that ran parallel to Richland Creek until they came to Waynesville.

In 1913 the route to town changed. The Methodists of

the Southeastern Jurisdiction purchased a large tract of land and dammed up Richland Creek to make Lake Junaluska and built a large Assembly Ground to accommodate summer conferences and gatherings of all kinds. Now Haywood County was obliged to build a "county road," a road that still goes by that name, so the rural residents of Crabtree, Fines Creek, and Iron Duff could get around the Methodists and go to town.

When the first service was held at the new Methodist Lake Junaluska Assembly, my father and grandfather were there. My grandfather was the North Carolina legislator from that part of the state and a lifelong Methodist as well. He took my Daddy with him, and they returned home telling of the beautiful new lake that was filling up and the assembly buildings that were under construction.

When I was growing up, we lived a mile and a half from Lake Junaluska, which had by then reached its maturity. In addition to conference and meeting facilities, there was a swimming pool, canoes to rent, a youth center with activities all summer, and there were summer-only kids my age from all over the Southeast for me to meet. Many of their families had second homes there or were at least vacationing with their families. I grew up first being taken to "the Lake" and then driving myself there when I became old enough.

In those days, there were entrance gates to the assembly grounds, and you needed to buy a gate pass for the time you were going to be there. Our family, being Methodist, always bought a season pass that admitted us not only to the grounds but also to the swimming pool and other organized activities.

By the time I was a junior in high school, I regularly haunted the pool and the youth center throughout the summer weeks. It was my playground, and though I never had an actual date with a Junaluska girl, I could at least watch and admire them freely!

There was an eleven o'clock curfew at the Lake during those summer weeks, and at 11:00 p.m., the gates were closed and locked. Everyone was supposedly settled until the following day. But—living nearby—I knew back ways to get in and out. At two or three places, tiny back roads, at that time unpaved, would take you from Methodist property back to the County Road. That way, I could be there past the eleven o'clock curfew and still get off the grounds when I decided to go home.

One night I had spent the entire evening at the Youth Center and had ended up leaving past curfew time. Knowing that the gates were closed and locked, I drove up past and around the old Terrace Hotel and was headed back toward the safety of County Road when a car blocked the road in front of me. About the time that I saw it, a red light started blinking on the top of the car. I knew who it was: the deputy sheriff for that part of Haywood County, a tall, large man whom everyone I knew called "Highpockets McElroy." He eased out and, flashlight in hand, approached my car.

"What are you doing back here, boy?" were his first words. "Don't you know that you're not supposed to be driving on the grounds after eleven o'clock? Let me see your driver's license."

"I'm on my way home," I sputtered. "I didn't mean to start out so late. I'm on my way home right now."

He shined the flashlight on my license and then looked at me. "It says you just live over in Waynesville. You're not even one of the summer people who are supposed to be here to start with. This place is for nice Methodists who come here to have meetings and get some rest for the summer. You don't even have any business being here ... you're nothing but a little old LOCAL BOY! Now get on home and don't be coming over here anymore."

So, feeling like a whipped dog with my tail between my legs, I slowly drove home and did not go back to my favorite place for the rest of that year. I felt shame and blame.

The coming year was my senior year in high school. With everything that happened that year at school, finishing high school, applying for college, and getting ready to leave home for the first time, I didn't have time to think about much else. I had been accepted to Davidson College in the springtime, and the rest of the school year, my head was filled with the possibilities and perils of that transition.

It was about the first of May when our family was in church one Sunday morning. We sat on the fourth row from the front on the right-hand side of the church, where we had been from the beginning of the world, I thought! I knew where everyone in church regularly sat; no one ever moved around from Sunday to Sunday.

When the service was over, our family was getting up to leave when Dr. Jim Fowler, the Superintendent of Lake Junaluska Assembly came across the aisles from the other side of the church where the Fowler family always sat. I guessed he needed to talk with my Daddy, so I paid no attention until he spoke to me.

"Donald," he started, "You're about to graduate, I know. What are you planning to do this summer before you go off to college?" Springtime had been so busy that I had not given summertime a thought. For the past two summers, I had worked at the Drive-In theatre and just assumed that I would be working there again.

"I'm not sure," I answered. "I'll be getting ready to go off to school and I don't have definite plans beyond that."

"Well," he continued, "I have a proposition for you. I got a phone call this week from Miss Stella Nance in Nashville; she's the manager of the Cokesbury Bookstore at Junaluska every summer. She told me that every time she tries to hire someone to work for her in the summer, she gets somebody who wants the job just so they can get to spend the summer at the Lake and that their social life gets to be more important than doing the job.

"She asked me if I could think about it and find her some good LOCAL BOY who already lives here who might be a good worker for her for the summer at the bookstore." He went on, "As soon as she asked that, I told her I had somebody in mind, and it was you. Do you want the job?"

I didn't have to think about it at all. Did I want a summer job working in a bookstore, and at Lake Junaluska, my favorite place, the place from which I feared I had been banned? *Of course,* I wanted the job. "I would love to work at the bookstore," was all I said, and it was done.

As soon as I was graduated from high school at the end of the month, the day arrived for me to report to the bookstore. Since we had no auditorium at Waynesville High School, my high school graduation had actually been held in the Stuart Auditorium at Lake Junaluska. Now I was going to be working right next door to where I was graduated and in one of my favorite places in the world.

On the determined day, I drove the mile and a half from home to Lake Junaluska and met Miss Stella Nance. She was a very old lady to still be working. In fact, later that summer, we had her *fiftieth* birthday celebration. I did not know people *that old* were still able to work, but she seemed up to the job.

The first thing we did was that she and I and Evelyn Joyner, her other employee for the summer, spent an entire day cleaning the empty store. It was two floors: the main floor, about 1,500 square feet, was where all the books were to be displayed and sold. The floor below was where we were to sell music, choir robes, brassware, pulpit robes, and other miscellaneous items for church use. The downstairs level also housed the small apartment where Miss Nance lived for the summer.

The following day we were to expect a U-Haul truck from Nashville bringing the stock for the summer. The truck came in late that night, and the next day, the driver unloaded box after box after box and wheeled them into the store. Under Miss Nance's direction, Evelyn and I opened each box and gradually filled the shelves, racks, and tables to set up the store.

This unloading, unpacking, and set-up took us nearly three days. Miss Nance directed us to move things from one place to another *several times* until she had all the stock set up exactly the way she wanted for the summer. I later realized that part of her strategy in the moving and rearranging was to be sure that we knew all the stock in the store, exactly where it was located, and even understood the logic of why it was arranged the way it was. She was quite a clever person, I gradually discovered.

The summer was to be twelve weeks of various meetings, conferences, and events, each week being different from the week before. The first big week was the meeting of the Western North Carolina Annual Conference of the Methodist Church, where business was conducted, and ministers were assigned for the coming year. We heard that there were about two thousand people at the Lake for that week, and I am sure that we saw every one of them more than once in the bookstore.

That first week, Miss Nance made something very clear to me. She told me that no one had ever worked more than a single summer for her. I was beginning to understand why. She was very critical of my work, something I had never experienced before. (Since Daddy was the loan officer at the bank, even my schoolteachers had been shy about criticism through my growing-up years.) I didn't really like the old lady!

As the summer rolled on, I learned about the various weeks and how they were different. There was Layman's Week, when we sold a large volume of books. There was Church Musicians' Week, when we sold very little since the musicians didn't have much money to spend. There was Ministers' Week, when almost all the sales were charged by the ministers back to the churches they served, and the Youth Weeks, when our stock didn't have much appeal to the teenagers.

One of the biggest weeks of the summer was called the Candler Camp Meeting. During that week, two well-known preachers were featured. The two would preach twice each day to packed crowds of ministers and lay people. The chosen ministers were usually people who had written several books, and we were sure that our store had all those books for sale during those busy weeks.

Sometime during the first week that I worked at the bookstore, Miss Nance casually again mentioned to the two of us who were working for her, "Do you know that no one has ever worked for me more than one summer." That was all that she said, just leaving us to think she was rubbing it in.

It turned out to be a wonderful summer! As time went on, I became more and more familiar with the stock. People could come into the store and ask for either a particular book or a certain kind of book. I had no trouble taking them straight to it.

Each week we received several boxes of new stock to both replenish what we had sold the last week and to bring in special items either on the topic of the week or written by those who were to be speakers during the coming weeks. On occasion, those shipments came on the big Overnight Freight truck, but more often, they came to the Post Office across the dam on the other side of the lake. Gradually, my job expanded to include driving to the Post Office to pick up those packages.

The Postmaster would call Miss Nance and let her know that we had three or four boxes to be picked up. Ms. Stella would then hand me her car keys and send me to do this favorite duty.

It was my favorite duty because the car she drove was a two-tone, green 1969 Oldsmobile Super 88 two-door hardtop. The car was so cool and so powerful! And I loved cars! It had the first power windows I had ever experienced in a car. I would take off, roll down all the windows, and hope that some young women might see me driving up over the hill by Lambeth Inn, down across the bridge at the dam, and up to the Post Office. Even if I had to load and unload four or five book boxes that could weigh forty-five or fifty pounds each, it was still a delight to get to make that little trip! I couldn't believe that such an old woman would drive such a *cool car.*

Working at the bookstore made me a part of the larger community of young people who worked at the Lake for the summer. Working there introduced me to a life that I had not experienced before. It was my first vision of a life that was not an extension of my parents, a time in which the choices and activities were mine and mine alone.

On Sundays, I sang in the Lake Junaluska Choir for the morning service at the big Stuart Auditorium. The director was the outgoing and inspiring Glenn Draper, who taught music at the University of Miami during the year and ran the music program at the Lake each summer for many, many years. Singing for Glenn was uplifting and inspiring as his choices, combined with the makeup of the large choir, gave me a sense of musical accomplishment and fulfillment.

(In recent years, I was in Chattanooga, Tennessee, for a storytelling festival. As one of the outreach programs of the festival, I was sent to do the luncheon program for one of the civic clubs. Before the meal started, it was Glenn Draper, now retired from the music department of the University of Chattanooga, who led a couple of songs and the National Anthem.

He retained the same energy that he displayed more than fifty years earlier!)

I also became a full participant in the summer Methodist Youth Programs at the Lake. These involved weekly Sunday night meetings, a Youth Activities Week, and several special outings and activities throughout the Summer.

There was also the highlighted Miss Junaluska pageant and all of its activities. I always joined the team of one of the "girls" running for Miss Junaluska and helped with the campaign activities. The whole summer was a new life of excitement for me. I felt that I had found a place where I belonged.

As the season came to an end, I remembered once again that Miss Nance had repeatedly told us no one had worked for her more than a single summer. I began to wonder whether I could find another job at the Lake for the following summer since that was where I really wanted to be, when she bluntly asked me, "Do you want to come back and work at the store again next summer?

Of course, the answer was a quick yes. I ended up working for her for five summers, from the summer after high school through the summer after my graduation from Davidson College.

The second summer at the bookstore was the beginning of a new adventure. Bill Finger came to join me working for Miss Nance. Bill and I were deeply into fun as well as work. We were both interested in young women, and gradually we developed several modes of private communication that allowed us to talk in code about those who came into the bookstore. If a woman was referred to as "fine" it meant that she was not attractive to us. But if a woman was "hurting," she was worth looking at more than once. The top honor was "really hurting."

Whenever a "really hurting" candidate came into the store at times when we were not busy (and especially at times when Miss Nance was not in the store to discipline us), we would try to see how long we could keep her in conversation so she would not leave the store. Interested in absolutely everything about our targets, we became gentle, champion interviewers.

One day we got an idea: what if we could devise a game to play with hurting women whom we wanted to keep in the store for our own entertainment? I think it was Bill who made a proposal.

"What if we ask a girl to think of a famous person. Then she whispers the name of that person to one of us. The one of us then starts to describe a trip they are going on. The first letter of each stop on the trip will spell out the name of the famous person and the other person will then tell the name." We began to try it out, *and it worked!*

If we got a name like "Eisenhower," the trip might be: "I woke up one morning in Iowa and decided to go to Kansas City by way of East St. Louis." Those first letters had already spelled out "IKE," and the answer was obvious to us but not to our victim.

The more we played, the more sophisticated the game became. There were a few famous people who got whispered repeatedly, like Abraham Lincoln. For these people, we developed codes rather than spelling out the entire name. The code for Lincoln was "five" since he was on the five-dollar bill.

We added more complications for those who wanted to "try again!" If we inserted a phrase like "on the second day," it meant that for the rest of that trip, it was the second letter in each destination that spelled out the answer. It became more and more difficult!

We had busy weeks and slow weeks as the summer progressed. Our busiest week was the Candler Camp Meeting. That summer, the preachers were Clovis Chappell and Wallace Hamilton. Wallace Hamilton had written a book or two, but Clovis Chappell had written thirty-eight books of sermons! We were selling his books like mad all week long, and we knew after that week that Clovis Chappell's sermons were being preached all over southeastern Methodism!

The following week was the slowest week of the summer: church musicians' week. The church musicians just didn't have any money to spend. They spent all day singing and not shopping. Besides that, it was dreary and rainy all week.

On one of those rainy afternoons, Miss Nance had left Bill and me to tend the store while she took the afternoon off.

There were no customers in the store, and we were descending into boredom when a very attractive young woman pushed the door open and came in out of the rain. She was carrying a folder in her hand. We both perked up, and Bill whispered, "She's hurting!"

She came over to the counter where we were and asked, "Do you guys happen to know where there is a piano I could practice on? I'm here with my family for a week's vacation and the house we are in doesn't have a piano. I need to practice instead of missing the whole week."

There was a piano in the back of our building in the adult center, and I volunteered to walk her back there and show her where it was. We walked back to the Adult Center, but the door was locked. There were no special activities going on that week, and the place had not even been opened up.

Sorry, she and I walked back to the store. By then, I knew her name, that she was a freshman at Columbia College, and where her family lived. When we got back to the store, Bill was waiting. "The piano is locked up.... There's no place to practice."

Bill took over, "Well, it sure is pouring rain. Why don't you stay in the store until it slows down. Hey ... want to play a game?" and we were on our way.

We played the "guess the famous person" game for about a half hour ... she would not give up on solving it. Then suddenly, she had a question for us: "Do you guys know how to

225

clog? Our family is going out to Maggie Valley to a square dance Saturday night, and I sure would like to know how to clog a little bit!"

I had grown up in the square dance world and Bill was quite a good clogger, so, we volunteered to give her clogging lessons right there in the bookstore. We had an old aquamarine-colored plastic-cased radio under the counter. We pulled it out and tuned in to WHCC where every afternoon's broadcast was a program they called "Cornbread Matinee," non-stop country and Bluegrass music my mother hated.

We turned the radio up loud (no customers were coming in the store, surely, while it was pouring rain like this) and started giving this "hurting" girl her first clogging lessons.

Bill and I were totally in control and having a wonderful time when, without any warning at all, the door opened, and a tall man dressed in a dark suit, white shirt, and tie walked into the store. We quickly killed the music and got both ourselves and our student calmed down.

"May I help you?" I asked. He looked like a Bishop or at least an important preacher to me.

"I'm looking for Miss Nance. Is she here?"

"No," I answered breathlessly. "She is out for the afternoon. Can I do anything to help you?"

He handed me a business card and continued, "You can tell her that I am up at the Terrace Hotel and that I am looking for her. Would you ask her to call me when she gets back?" As

226

he stiffly turned to leave, I looked at the card he had handed me. It read: "Lovick Pierce, President, The Methodist Publishing House, Nashville, Tennessee." All the blood drained out of my head. This was the big boss of all big bosses, not only our boss, but Miss Nance's boss as well.

Mr. Pierce turned and walked out the door into the rain and left us alone in the store. The young woman left in a hurry perceiving that something bad had just happened. Bill and I were quiet for a long time and didn't have much to say to one another.

Near the end of the afternoon, Miss Nance came back to the store to see how we were doing and to tell us we should close at seven instead of eight since nothing was happening today. I told her, "A man came looking for you this afternoon.... He left this card for you. He said that he is staying over at the Terrace Hotel, he wants to see you." She took the card and looked at it.

"Mr. Pierce.... Oh my gosh ... I had no idea he was coming. What in the world is he doing here? He has never been to this store before! I better walk up there and see what this is all about," and she left us.

She was gone almost no time. When she came back into the store, she had a very serious look on her face. She told Bill he should take break time. Once he was out of the store, she turned to face me.

"Donald," she started, "You can go ahead and leave now. You can come back on Monday and pick up your last check."

I was fired on the spot.

I had no idea what this was all about.… Or maybe I did. I was sure that Mr. Pierce had ordered her to fire me because of the way Bill and I were behaving when he walked into the store unannounced. I wondered if Bill was going to be fired also when he got back from his break.

I got in my car and slowly drove around until it was the normal time to arrive home. I did not say one word to my parents about being fired; on Friday and Saturday, I went over to my friend David's house, and he and I spent two days together. I did not tell him that I was fired either, just that I had some time off.

I went over to the store early Monday morning to get my last check knowing that she would have it written so that she would not have to see me again. When I walked up to the door, she was looking for me. As I pushed the door open, she said, "I'm glad you are here early ... this is going to be Layman's Week, and we are always busy this week. These Laymen have plenty of money to spend, and we will be staying open until after the evening service is finished every day to get them as they go back to their rooms. How about taking my car and going over to the Post Office.… I know we've got a shipment of new books for the week." And so, I was hired again on the spot.

Never after this day did either one of us say a single word about what had happened. I never said a word about it to Bill and never learned whether he had also been temporarily fired like I was or not.

That was the last summer I worked at the bookstore. At the end of the summer, I entered Duke University Divinity School, and the following summers were spent doing fieldwork assignments from the Divinity School.

By now, Stella Nance had become a dear friend, and I always stopped by the bookstore to visit her anytime I went home to Waynesville at the beginning and end of summer. When I got married, she sent a beautiful engraved red leather Bible that I treasure to this day.

Years rolled on. I finished at Duke and took my first appointment as a United Methodist minister, eventually spending twenty-five years in that calling before I retired in 1990 to spend all my time in the world of storytelling.

The Nashville, Tennessee, area would often be a stop on the storytelling circuit. I might be in Nashville itself or in surrounding towns like Lebanon, Murfreesboro, or Franklin. In her retirement, Stella lived in her old family hometown of Smyrna, Tennessee. Somehow every time I ended up in her part of the world, she would find out about it and would show up at my performances. She always had to be sure that the audience members seated close to her knew that she "trained me" and that we were really family members.

It happened that my wedding anniversary and her

birthday fell on the same day, August 26, so on that day, we always talked by telephone and caught up on old memories. I also stopped by her house in Smyrna for longer visits.

It was August of 1997. When the twenty-sixth rolled around, I called her as usual, and we had our birthday/anniversary visit on the phone. All of a sudden, in the middle of the call she said, "I have been thinking a lot about those days in the bookstore lately for some reason. In fact, I climbed up in the attic last week and found a whole lot of stuff from those Junaluska days."

Then, out of nowhere, the question hit me, "Do you remember when Mr. Pierce came?" I almost dropped the phone.

When I recovered myself, I answered, "I sure do."

She went on, "I never did tell you what that was all about." I was about to hear a story that I might have never heard in my life, a story that informed the depth of a friendship and filled me with a sense of appreciation I would never have had without hearing it.

"Do you remember that the week before we had had the Candler Camp Meeting? Do you also remember that we had the 'A-B-or C' key on the cash register that we each would hit when we made a sale to show who made the sale in case there was a problem later? Well, when the sales records for the Camp Meeting week went into the main office in Nashville, they showed that whoever 'B' was had not only made the most sales that week, but whoever 'B' was had made more sales that week than any permanent salesperson in any year-round store in the entire Publishing House system. You were "B."

"So, Mr. Pierce had made a special trip to Lake Junaluska to try to hire *you* to come to work full-time in Nashville with the Publishing House. Now just think about that; you were in love with books and with working at the bookstore. You would have taken that job offer.

"I, on the other hand, knew that working for the publishing house was too small for what you should live up to in your life. I had heard you tell stories for five summers there in the bookstore without even knowing what you were doing, and I knew that you were supposed to write books, not sell them.

"So," she finished her story, "I found out how long Mr. Pierce was going to be at Junaluska, and I fired you for that long so he couldn't find you. You were twenty-two years old, and I knew a lot better than you did what was good for you. You can thank me now!"

In February, following that telephone conversation, my dear friend, Stella Nance, died. Had we not had that conversation back in August, I would never have known that Mentor used to drive a green Super 88 Oldsmobile.

Chapter Fourteen

Ginger Olson

SPECIAL NOTE: The following story happened fifty years ago, and it was still extremely difficult for me to write. It will be hard for you to read. Skip it if you have doubts. But, it is about a person, Ginger Olson, who deserves to be remembered. So, I am writing this note without apology. Read with respect and care.

In 1969, the week of my twenty-fifth birthday, I graduated from Duke Divinity School. I had been ordained a Deacon two years earlier and was now supposed to be prepared to be a United Methodist Minister.

Having no experience and needing to serve a probationary year under supervision before I could receive my final ordination as an Elder, I was assigned to be an Associate Minister at First United Methodist Church in High Point, North Carolina.

After that year, my probationary time was up. I was ordained an Elder and given the first assignment where I was the pastor in charge of my own churches. Actually, there were two of them. As was quite normal in Methodism, I was appointed to what was called a "two-point charge," two small churches served by one minister.

My churches, Wesley Heights and St. Timothy's United Methodist Church, were located on either side of Lexington, North Carolina. Each Sunday, I conducted worship services at St. Timothy's at 9:30 and then drove about three miles across town to lead the service at Wesley Heights at 11:00 o'clock.

The people in these churches were kind and patient with me, a young and inexperienced minister who knew much less than most of them did about what a minister was supposed to do and how a church was supposed to be run. They taught me a great deal and perhaps enabled me to teach them a little bit in return for their patience.

It was Palm Sunday of 1973. The date was April 15. After a late spring, this day was the first truly warm, sunny day when it felt like winter had lost its last grip and spring was here to stay. After church, the youth group went to eat at Lexington Barbeque with a few parents, and then we all had a long bike ride out in the country on the west side of town. It was a glorious day. Everyone seemed relaxed.

After the bike ride, we were sitting in the backyard of the parsonage with Randy and Beth Parlier from across the street.

They were two members of our youth group at the church. The Smith kids from down the street were also hanging around. We heard a sound and looked toward it to see a police car pull up into the driveway.

This caused no concern. Karen and Petey Smith's dad was a policeman. Maybe he was on the way home and saw them hanging out there. I started to walk over toward the police car when the door opened. A policeman I did not know got out on the driver's side, and George Mauney got out on the other side. George was a church member and neighbor but also the Assistant Chief of Police and head of the Detective Division. They both looked very glum.

As they came up the driveway and into the backyard, the kids scattered and headed home. I was left there alone when George spoke up: "Preacher, would you happen to know where the Doswell Olsons are? They are members over at St. Timothy's, aren't they?"

The Olson family had joined St. Timothy's, the smaller church on the other side of town, maybe a year or so before. They had come to Lexington from the Washington, DC, area. Mr. Olson, who went by "Ollie," worked for the Rural Electrification Authority, and a job reassignment moved their whole family to town.

There were three children: Ginger was the oldest and a college freshman. Karen was a middle-schooler, and Karl was a bit younger than that. They had become strong and active members of this small church where every member made a great difference, and everyone was like family.

George went on, "They don't seem to be at home. None of the neighbors seem to be home either, so we couldn't ask them. Did they come to church this morning?"

In my mind, I was remembering that, no, the Olsons were not at church that morning. I already knew that without thinking. The Sunday before, as they came out the door at the end of the service, Mrs. Olson had told me, "We will not be here for the next two Sundays. We are leaving at the end of the week to go visit my parents in Missouri. We'll see you when we get back." I had told her that we would miss them and hoped that they would have safe travels. That was the end of the conversation.

I relayed this information to George. "Do you have any idea where that might be, or anything about her parents? We need to find them." All this time, I was trying to simply blank out my mind from speculating about what was going on. Whatever it was, I did not think that I wanted to know about it.

Suddenly I realized something. Sometime in the past year, Mrs. Olson's parents had come to visit and had come to church with them. I told George this and then offered, "There may be a chance that they signed the guest register when they came to church. Do you want to ride over there and check it out?" He agreed that we should give it a try and opened the back door of the police car for me to get in.

The officer, who was his driver, started the car, and we backed out of the driveway. No one said a word on the drive across town to St. Timothy's Church. None of us seemed to want to say anything. I wondered what they were thinking and dared to guess what had happened.

We got to the church and pulled into the parking lot. I pulled out the key, and the three of us went inside. There, just inside the door of the sanctuary building, was the guest register on a wooden stand. We walked over to it, and I flipped back for about a year and began to read the entries. I was moving very slowly as if I could put off the inevitable information that they were still withholding from me.

Suddenly I stopped looking. There in the guest register were the names for which we were looking: "Mr. and Mrs. Hulet Woods, Dexter, Missouri." Now we knew the town where they lived. This was what George was looking for. He wrote down the information, and we started walking back to the car.

Suddenly George spoke to me. "We might as well tell you what's going on. You're going to be right in the middle of it pretty soon. The daughter is dead." I remember those were his exact words: *the daughter is dead.* I do not think he knew the makeup of the family, and he had no names to go with this information.

The Olsons had two daughters. Which one could it be?

There was Karen, the middle-schooler whom I assumed had made the trip with her parents along with their even younger son, Karl. Then there was Ginger. Ginger had recently graduated from High School and was a student at the University of North Carolina in Asheville.

My mind went immediately to automobile accidents. When I was a student at Davidson College, my freshman roommate had been killed in a car accident along with another student who lived in our hall. This must be what I was on the verge of learning about. Not so.

George did not say anything until we got back into the car and started back across town. He was letting information out just a little bit at a time. "She was murdered ... I guess you would call it that. They found her body tied up in the Botanical Gardens up there where she was going to school in Asheville." The reality of his words began slowly to sink in.

By the time I got back home, the phone was ringing. The death had hit television news in Asheville, and people who knew that I lived in Lexington were calling, not knowing how close I was to this family.

Ginger was a very quiet girl, surely on the introverted side of personalities. She was petite and attractive. Just the summer before, she had volunteered to be a counselor with me for our joint churches' day camp. We had worked closely together for that week, and I had learned a lot about her.

She was a drama major. She told me that when she was on the stage, she felt safe. Up there, she could disappear into the play itself. It was very different from trying to have a face-to-face conversation with someone back on the ground. I understood this very well. The most uncomfortable time for me in church was not when I was preaching but when I had to speak to everyone personally as they came out the door when it was all over. I understood her.

She also had worked as a lifeguard at the community swimming pool located just at the end of the street from where we lived. It was the pool where we went with our small son, Douglas, and where all the kids from the churches would hang out through summer vacation.

My assumption was that George was in touch with the Asheville Police Department in an attempt to locate the Olsons. I later discovered that the task had been passed to Peter Gilpin, the Publicity Director at the University of North Carolina at Asheville. It was Peter who got the information and was charged with calling Ginger's grandparent's home searching for her parents. And it was Peter's wife who took upon herself the task of eventually informing Ginger's mother about what had happened to her child.

While all this was happening, the Asheville Police and the North Carolina State Bureau of Investigation were moving as quickly as they could to try to solve Ginger's murder.

On the Friday before Palm Sunday, the Olsons had left Lexington and driven up to Asheville. They spent the night there, and on Saturday, visited with Ginger before driving toward Dexter, Missouri.

On Sunday morning, Ginger and her roommate, Jane Nicholson, slept late. About 12:00 or 12:30, Ginger gathered her Spanish book and notebook and headed out to the botanical garden to study on that first warm day of spring. Jane, whose parents were coming over from Brevard, North Carolina, for a visit, did not go with Ginger on this day.

At about 3:30 that afternoon, two teenagers, Thomas Guthrie, age fourteen, and Larry O'Kelly, age seventeen, were returning from picnicking in the woods beyond the botanical gardens. They came upon Ginger's body, stabbed to death, and tied up with her own clothing, lying in the middle of the well-traveled path. They had heard no screams or other sounds prior to their discovery. Later tests showed that she had been killed instantly by the initial stab wound to her heart.

At this time and even later that day, when George Mauney had come to find me seeking the location of her parents, the Olsons were still driving toward Missouri. In those pre-cell-phone days, there was no way to contact them on the road. Mrs. Olson's parents, the Woods, were contacted but not told what had happened, just that there was an emergency. It was after their later arrival that Peter Gilpin's wife finally caught them up on what had happened to their daughter.

Back home in Lexington, I was trying to figure out what I, as the minister to the Olson family, needed to do and could do at this time. I spent a couple of days of waiting and making long-distance phone calls trying to keep up with events and potential funeral plans.

On Monday, the Olsons flew from Missouri to Asheville, where they were met by police and university officials. They were, at last, filled in on the whole story and were taken to identify Ginger's body. Gradually, plans were made.

The family received visitors at Anders-Rice Funeral home on Tuesday evening. A memorial service was planned to be held on the campus on Wednesday. After that, Mr. and Mrs. Olson would fly back to Missouri and get their car before meeting her body in Parsons, Tennessee, where she would be buried in a family plot at the New Prospect Baptist Church cemetery.

I traveled up to Asheville on Tuesday to meet with them and to be part of the memorial service on Wednesday in a packed auditorium on the campus. By now, her boyfriend, Jeff Doyle, a student at William and Mary, had arrived in Asheville and had joined the Olson family. Wednesday was a very long day as the service was held in late morning, and by that afternoon, I was on the way back to Lexington.... It was Holy Week with upcoming Maundy Thursday services and then Easter services on Sunday.

Before cell phones, I had no contact with the Olsons as we went our separate ways. They faced full days of deep mourning, encased in the responsibilities of funeral and transportation logistics. I had to return to all the Holy Week events and move forward through Easter. We would see one another at some unstated time when they were back home, and this had all settled down a bit.

Planning for church services for Easter was very difficult following Ginger's death. It was all that was on the minds of everyone in Lexington. Questions, many of them theological, filled the atmosphere as Sunday approached. I decided that the best thing for me to do was to simply retell the whole Easter story from passion through resurrection and let it stand on its own.

On Sunday morning, I headed across town to St. Timothy's early enough to arrive there before anyone else did, as was my habit. But when I pulled into the church parking lot, there was another car already there. It was a blue Dodge that looked amazingly like the blue Dodge driven by the Olsons. I knew that it could not be since Ginger's burial service had been the afternoon before in Tennessee, but as I approached the car, the window rolled down, and, indeed, the Olson family was there, waiting for the church hour to arrive. I saw Mr. and Mrs. Olson in the front seat with Karl and Karen in the back. As I leaned down to see them, sitting there with tears in their eyes, I said something stupid, like, "I didn't expect to see you here today."

Mr. Olson quietly replied, "Oh, we had to be here today. You see, this is the first time we have ever needed Easter … because this was the first time we ever experienced Good Friday." There was nothing more to be said.

Others arrived and greeted them mostly in silence. I simply read the whole story from chapters 26-28 in Matthew's gospel, from Jesus' announcement of his death through the resurrection. It was enough.

The crime was never solved. The only physical evidence at the scene was a piece of flesh not belonging to Ginger that was impaled on a tree branch. Everything else there belonged to her.

The day after her death, a young man was taken in under suspicion after he was caught breaking and entering in the neighborhood. He was released after alibis established no possible connection.

Other anecdotal stories came up in the weeks following. One often repeated account was that a young adult male whose family home was in the vicinity had recently been released from a mental institution. When the police attempted to question him, they discovered that his family had just moved him to another institution in Canada where he could not be questioned.

Both the Asheville Police and the State Bureau of Investigation continued to pursue every possible lead to discover who was involved in Ginger's death. Not one single lead ever led to solving the mysteries of that afternoon. The case is still open to this day.

We later had another memorial service for Ginger at St. Timothy's Church for friends and neighbors in Lexington. By this time, a lot of stories about Ginger had been told. I shared some that I had heard and ended the service with this memory:

"Ginger wrote things: notes, notebooks, verses, personal thoughts, and feelings. On top of the desk in her room at school was found a paper on which she had written the following lines. They tell us more about who she was and the kind of person she sought to be than anything else I can say:

TODAY

1. I will be happy.
2. Adjust myself to what is.
3. Exercise, care for, and nourish my body.
4. Strengthen my mind.
5. Do somebody a good turn and not be found out— do two things I do not want to.
6. I will be agreeable, dress becomingly, talk low, act courteously, praise others, and try not to improve or regulate anyone else.
7. Deal with today.
8. Will have a program.
9. Quiet time, a time of prayer, Bible reading.
10. Try to relax and not worry.

11. Just for today, I will be unafraid, especially I will not be afraid to be happy, to enjoy what is beautiful, to love—to believe those I love, love me.

12. Also ... John 3:16.

This story may be the only tangible memory that is left of her in this world. I leave it because I think she deserves to be lovingly remembered.

Chapter Fifteen

The Wheelers

BEING UNITED METHODIST, at the Annual Conference of 1973, I was assigned to a new parish. The assignment was to be the Director of the Cherokee County United Methodist Parish in that last far-western eponymous county in the mountains of North Carolina. We were to live in Andrews, North Carolina, where I would be mainly centered around the church in the middle of town while also having a multitude of responsibilities related to the other two pastoral charges in Cherokee County.

I was twenty-nine years old with a wife, a child, and no money. So, we did not make a trip ahead of time to see where we were going to live and first saw the town of Andrews on the day when we moved there.

It was about five hours from Lexington, the town we were leaving. We left in the early morning with my wife, Beth, driving our Opel station wagon with our two-year-old son, Douglas. I followed, driving the twenty-two-foot U-Haul truck that we had rented to take everything we owned from our old home to our new one. We had not even seen the parsonage in which we were to live.

In 1973 Andrews was a charming little town. It was just enough farther back in the mountains to feel like my hometown of Waynesville during my growing-up childhood there. I felt comfortably at home as soon as we drove into town.

We looked briefly at the church, right there on the main street of the little town, but mostly we needed to find the parsonage and get the rental truck unloaded so we could turn it in and not pay for an extra day. We were met by Mr. John Christy and directed to the parsonage.

This house, in which we were to live for the coming five years, had been built in 1959. It was a light-colored brick with 1959 turquoise wood trim. It was not a split-level house. No, it was a tri-level house that looked as if it might run down the sloping hill on which it was built. As soon as I saw the house, the only thing I could think about was the eight-hundred-pound upright grand piano that was riding in the back of the U-Haul truck. That piano was going to need to go into the top of the three levels of the house, a good stretch above the driveway where the truck was destined to be unloaded.

A quick decision was made. We would back the truck into the driveway so we could go ahead and unload everything into the garage on the bottom level. Then the truck could be returned, and all that stuff in the garage would hopefully gradually find its way upstairs as time allowed.

The truck was mostly unloaded, and the piano had just been lowered with the hydraulic lift when the first curious neighbor came walking across the yard to introduce himself. It was a young man, well over six feet tall, with wide shoulders and a shock of hair that could not honestly be called red since it was properly closer to orange. He also had freckles on top of freckles and freckles crowding out other freckles. We met Joe Wheeler.

Joe had grown up in the house just behind us, where he lived with his mother while he studied at Western Carolina University fifty miles away. While we visited with Joe, I began to look at his size and have guilty feelings about the possibility of getting his help to move the piano from the driveway up to the living room of the house. But, no, I thought ... not when we have just met ... that would not be right.

All of a sudden, a second person walked across the yard toward us. He was as tall as Joe and built the same way but with brown hair and no freckles. It was Joe's little brother, Jack, a student at the University of North Carolina in Chapel Hill.

As I was meeting Jack and the three of us continued to talk, the piano came to mind again. This time I couldn't help myself. "Hey guys," I started. "So, you think you could help me do something ... it won't take long. See this piano? It needs to go up into the living room. Do you think you could help me roll it out to the street and up to the sidewalk and then get it inside the house? It has wheels!"

Joe instantly replied for both of them: "I'll go get Mama!" He disappeared back across the yard and, in about five minutes, reappeared with Mama Ruth, a living lesson in genetic consistency.

As soon as she saw the piano, she gave the orders: "The three of you get that end and I'll get this end." By then, she was already picking up her end of the big piano while the boys and I lifted our end. We were on the way.

About halfway up to the front door, the three of us tried to put our end down and rest. Mama Ruth wouldn't have it. "Don't stop now, boys, we've got it going." In no time, we had the piano installed in the living room, where it would remain for the next five years.

That is the day we met the Wheelers, our back-door neighbors for those coming years. Very soon, we met Guinn, the boys' older brother, and Maxine, their only sister.

As time moved forward, we grew closer and closer to Mama Ruth and Joe. They were the permanent neighbors, there all the time, as Guinn and Maxine lived elsewhere, and Jack went back to college at the end of the summer.

When you become part of someone's life, you gradually learn their story. The Wheelers were no exception. Part of the story came from them directly, and part of it was community-shared information.

Ruth's husband, the children's father, had been the meat cutter at the local independent grocery store. He was also a serious alcoholic. One day Mr. Wheeler did not come home from work after the store closed. In a little while, Ruth went down to see where he was, already having suspicions about what she might possibly find. When she entered the unlocked back door of the meat market at the store, she discovered that, instead of coming home, her husband had committed suicide there in the store after everyone else had gone home.

Up to that point in her life, with four young children, Ruth had been a stay-at-home mother. They never owned a home, always being renters in a family with an unreliable breadwinner. Now that her husband was dead and she was in charge, everything changed. Ruth got a job at the Baker Furniture plant where she learned to carve ornate headboards for expensive beds the likes of which she would never own. She built and paid for their first house, raised four children, and sent three of them to college, all without any help from anyone but the children and herself.

When I finally came to understand that story, I wanted to know more from her about how she had managed to do all those things. One day we were out in the yard between our two gardens when I finally asked her, "Ruth, you know that I know about your husband and your whole family. Now Guinn and Maxine are grown up and Joe and Jack are in college. You have your job and your house. All by yourself, how did you manage to do all of that?"

With a sly grin, she thought for a moment, then answered: "I did it all in one day."

I had to know more.

"That day, when I came back up from the store and knew we were on our own, I knew that if we were going to make it as a family, we were going to have to be a family that knew how to vote." Then she left me standing there and headed for her house in a way that told me she was not finished with me and that I needed to stay right there until I learned what she now meant for me to know.

In only a couple of minutes, she returned from her house holding a folded piece of paper in her hands. Even folded, it looked worn, like it had been refolded and handled many, many times. As she unfolded the paper, she held it out for me to see.

The unfolded paper displayed three sets of words in large print. They were:

HAPPY OR SAD...
RICH OR POOR...
SICK OR WELL...
LIVE OR DIE.

I understood that this paper was their family ballot. Ruth proceeded to explain it all to me. "You see, every day when we had breakfast, as a family, we would get out this paper, read these words out loud, and vote on what the day was going to be like. Do you know that once you vote on it, once you make that decision, that's the way the day turns out? You just make it that way."

Joe and Jack had slightly different versions of things. Joe stated it, "She raised us using a big Arm and Hammer Baking Soda box. She would get that soda box out in the morning and hold it up for us to see. Then she would flex her biceps and tell us that the picture on the soda box was her arm. She would then set the soda box on the kitchen counter, where we would see it first thing when we got home from school while she was still at work. With the soda box in its proper place, she would look at us and say: 'When you get home from school, do your homework, clean up the house, and fix supper.'" He told me that he tried to run from her once, and that was all!

We didn't see Joe's sister, Maxine, very often. She lived pretty far away and only showed up for a visit periodically. Jack would be there in the summer when he was out of school, but once school started for him in Chapel Hill, he was gone until the holidays came.

Guinn, their older brother (his given name was Ruth's maiden name), came around regularly. Guinn had suffered some mild oxygen deprivation at birth, and—though he could drive and hold down a job—he had developed a marvelously hilarious personality. He would cock his eye, listen to what was going on, grin, and come out with one-liners that would break up the whole party.

There were many "Guinn stories" in the neighborhood, but it was Dr. F. E. Blaylock who told me the funniest one. It seems that, during the Vietnam War era, Guinn had received his draft notice and, as was the practice in that small town, was directed to report to Dr. Blaylock for a preliminary physical. Dr. Blaylock told me that he knew Guinn did not belong in the armed services, but he needed a solid reason to classify him as ineligible.

Guinn knew that he was being examined with the possibility of going into the Army and being sent to a place called Vietnam. Dr. Blaylock began to ask him the required set of questions that led to the physical examination. When he got to the question that asked, "Can you swim?" Guinn burst out with laughter and hooted, "Ain't they got no boats?" Guinn was kindly informed by Dr. Blaylock that he had been chosen to stay home and work instead of going into the Army.

It was Ruth and Joe to whom we were the closest. Probably because they were always there, with Ruth working at Baker Furniture each day and Joe driving over to Cullowhee for classes at the same time. Gradually our house became Joe's major hang-out. Joe walked in and out of our doors without ever thinking about knocking.

Our first year in Andrews was Joe's last college year at

Western Carolina. When he graduated in June, he almost immediately got a job right at home in Cherokee County as a Social Services Case Worker for the elderly.

Joe was a wonderful social worker and a natural with his older clients. But he couldn't quite keep the rules. He just could not refuse to give them his home telephone number. Sometimes late in the night or into the early morning hours, I would hear his little orange Ford Fiesta cranking up. This seemed to happen most often when the weather was most dreary. I might rise up in bed and look from our upper floor down toward the Wheeler house and watch Joe's little car back out of the driveway. I knew that I would hear the story the next day, never with names attached, about how one of his clients just needed him a little bit. Maybe they were sick or scared or drunk … or perhaps just too lonely. He poured his life into his work.

As time unfolded, we had three little boys in that house, and Joe was, for all of them, their best friend. Whenever they would see him coming over through the yard toward our house, they would run up to him all together, shouting, "Let's play Merry-Go-Round!" Jonathan would end up on his shoulders with hands full of orange hair while Kelly and Douglas each grabbed a hand. They would run round and round while Joe started spinning wildly until the boys were off the ground. Finally, they all fell to the ground in a dizzy heap, yelling, "Let's do it again!" They never tired of playing with Joe.

One day, very soon after we moved to Andrews, Joe came over to the house with an idea. "Do you know," he started, "about the John Campbell Folk School?"

I did indeed know about the Folk School. When I was in the eighth grade, our teacher, Mr. Roy Haupt, spent his Saturdays (along with his wife, Susan) taking students on personal field trips around Western North Carolina. Most of those trips were related to his hobby, rock and mineral collecting. On one of those trips, we were taken to Copper Hill, Tennessee, and on the way back, we made a detour outside Murphy, North Carolina, to go to the Folk School.

Founded in 1925 by Olive Dame Campbell and Marguerite Bidstrup, the Danish-style Folk School offered non-credit courses for adults in a wide range of arts and crafts. It was also the home of many community music and dance events. Now I realized that we lived less than twenty miles from that wonderful community asset.

Joe continued, "You know that they have a community dance every Saturday night. There is also a dance class on Tuesdays. Why don't we all go? Mama could either stay here with the boys, or we could all go, and she could be in charge of them while we dance."

That very Saturday night, we headed to the Folk School, all of us, and we seldom ever missed either a Saturday dance or a Tuesday class.

Dance at the Folk School included English Country

Dance, Contras and Squares, and Danish dance. We had wonderful fun, and it was a great contrast from the work of each week. We would get to the dance, and the music would warm up. Then the caller for the evening would take the microphone and announce, "Everybody take a partner and make a big circle, and we'll get started. You don't need to know anything for this dance.... You only need to take a partner."

In the 1970s, "take a partner" meant, "Men, ask a woman to dance." With that instruction, each man moved quickly, sometimes knocking into others, trying to get to the attractive woman he had chosen as his hoped-for partner. Joe just sat there and didn't hurry. When everything was settled down, and the circle was forming, he would then get up, walk across the floor, and ask one of the remaining women least likely to ever be asked if they would like to dance. After he set that exemplary pattern, everyone danced. (And he was so big ... he could swing partners off the floor who hadn't left the ground since childhood!)

The Folk School became a second home for us as a community, friend base, and center of artistic meaning.

One day Joe came over to the house with a new idea: "I've read that Jack Hall is starting a new course over at the Folk School on carving wooden animals. I've always wanted to do that. How about if you and I go over and sign up for the course? It's going to be on Thursday nights."

The following Thursday, Joe and I drove over to the Folk School and signed up for the course. We met with Jack Hall (who has carvings in the Smithsonian), and he led us through our introductory session with knives and wood. Joe and I discovered that we were so very talented that on that very first night, we both learned to carve fingers! We decided that the class was not for us. However, we had gained so much appreciation for the talents of those who could carve, seemingly effortlessly, that we didn't even ask for our money back as we withdrew from the course.

I think it was after this experience that Joe began to collect carved wooden animals. He would save up a little bit of money from his check each month, stop by the gift shop at the Folk School when we went over to dance, and buy matched pairs of all the kinds of animals he found there. Eventually, I discovered what he was doing when, one day, he asked for my help. He was collecting sets of paired animals for a Noah's Ark set, and he wanted me to help him build the ark.

I did have a power saw in the garage and some scraps of pretty nice cherry wood, so, we went at it. Joe drew the plan, and I cut it out. Then we both crudely nailed and glued the ark together. It was complete with a large wooden gangplank for the animals to parade up as they happily and cooperatively lined up to enter the ark. We put the finished ark on the coffee table in Mama Ruth's living room, and the animals continued to grow in number as it rested there.

There was one time when Joe saved my life. It all started on a bright day in the fall of the year when I was out in the yard talking with Mama Ruth. While we were talking, a pickup truck came past loaded with firewood. It slowed down, and the driver yelled out the window, "Do y'all want to buy any firewood? It's hickory and white oak, and it's dried out."

Ruth looked at me and offered, "I'll go half a load with you if you want the other half." There was a large brick fireplace in our house, but I had never thought of building a fire in it the winter before.

"Does our fireplace work?" I asked. "Do you know?"

"The people who lived there before used it. I used to see smoke coming out the chimney all the time."

"Okay," I agreed. "I'll go halves with you," and, with that, I had a good stack of dried firewood.

As the season wore on and the days began to get cooler, I kept waiting for the right chance to try out what, to me, was the "new" fireplace. Finally, a crisp, clear, cool day came that was just right. I went home for lunch and after eating, laid a fire in the fireplace and struck a match to the kindling. The fire caught immediately, but all the smoke came pouring out into the living room with nothing at all going up the chimney.

Then I remembered what I had noticed when we moved in the year before but had totally forgotten. A metal sheet covered the chimney, and a brick on top held it in place. You could see it from the yard if you just looked up. It had been designed to keep the chimney swifts from nesting there. I headed out the door in a panic but had no plan in mind.

Right beside the door of this 1959 house, there was a brick-framed flower bed and an open-work brick trellis that extended in a decorative way from the brickwork of the house itself. The openwork of the trellis was sized just right to be hand and foot holds. In no time, I had clambered up the trellis, got on top of the roof of the house, tossed the brick and the metal chimney cover to the ground, and sat down with relief that the smoke was all now coming right up and out the chimney.

Then...I realized that I now had to get back down. No one else was at home for some reason, so there was no help to call on. I went back over and looked down at the trellis I had just climbed with the help of panic and adrenalin and realized that there was no possible way I could ever get back down that way. There was nothing to do but sit and wait until someone came along who could help me get down to the ground.

By now, it was afternoon, and workers from the Baker Furniture plant were headed home on the shortest route from the plant to town, which happened to be right past the house. As I sat on the roof, most of them looked over at me and smiled and waved like they assumed it was simply a natural choice for me to sit up on the housetop all afternoon.

Finally, Joe's car turned the corner, and he was home from work. He didn't see me immediately, so I yelled out to him. He looked all around toward all the places where he might expect to see me until I yelled again, and he finally looked up to where I was stuck on the roof.

Before he had a chance to say his first word, I blurted out, "Don't laugh! Just help me get down from here."

Joe tried not to laugh as he walked all around the back of the house, assessing the situation. "Let me see if I can find a ladder. Do you happen to have one?"

"No." My answer was disappointing even to me.

"Let me look over at the house." In a few minutes, Joe returned, but not with a ladder. With no ladder to be found, he had brought Mama Ruth's three-step kitchen stool. He had it unfolded and resting on his shoulders with the top step a couple of feet above his head.

"I'll get close to the house. You slide off the roof and land on this. I'll catch you." There was no other option. Joe got near the corner of the house where the yard sloped up instead of down, braced himself, and I reluctantly slid off the roof and landed right on the stool as he had promised. There was no laughter ... just snickering smiles.

After that, every time we had a fire in the fireplace, it seemed like a well-earned pleasure.

There was only one occasion on which I thought I might have been in danger of losing Joe's friendship. It was a cold Christmas Eve in the mountains when Joe came over to the house a little while after all the boys were in bed to ask whether

Santa Claus needed any help before the next day. I told him that Santa Claus did indeed need some help. Hidden in the garage on the bottom level of the house, packaged in a long rectangular box, were all the components of a new swing set that had been requested of Santa. We had to work very quietly to get all the pieces out into the yard without making a lot of clanging noise. Then, in the cold of that Christmas Eve night, Joe and I discovered by flashlight that the assembly directions were written in some kind of oriental script that we could not even identify, let alone understand.

Still, he stuck with it and helped me, there in the freezing dark, until we had all the pieces screwed and bolted together ... in the right order! The next morning, everyone awakened with a happy surprise on an unusually warm Christmas day filled with swinging and happy climbing. Joe never complained one word about it; he loved our family so much that he would have helped all night to keep the little boys from being disappointed.

Our friendship had been growing for nearly a half-dozen years when, one Saturday night after the community dance, Joe gathered everyone together before anyone had a chance to leave. He had an announcement to make.

"I quit my job this week," he started. "I'm moving to Atlanta."

We all knew that, for some time now, Joe had been struggling with particular identity issues. But it was the nineteen-seventies, and sexual identity was just not something that people had learned to talk openly about. Honesty was regarded as an even more private issue.

"Yes," he went on. "I'm leaving this week. I've got an apartment there and a good line on a job." No one asked any questions. We hugged him goodbye with sadness for our own loss, but we all knew that Joe was simply going to look for Joe.

And so, I lost living next door to a very dear and almost family-member friend.

Once in a while, I would be talking with Mama Ruth in the yard, and I would ask about Joe. "Oh," she reported to me one day, "He's fine. He's a banker." She went on to tell me that Joe had a job working at night opening people's credit card payments and punching them into a machine. "He's a banker." I knew that was the way mamas tell the story.

About a year after that, I was moved to a new assignment in Charlotte, North Carolina, and, with that, my close connection with the Wheelers became one of memories.

Nearly ten years later, I took a retired relationship with the church and moved into full-time work as a traveling storyteller. The first Christmas in this new life found a large, square Christmas card waiting to be opened. It had no return address, as was not uncommon with Christmas cards. When I opened it, years melted away with the surprise of good memories. It was from Joe! His note simply said, "Dear Donald, I am so glad to learn that you are finally free to tell all of your stories."

Then I knew that even though I could not see him, he was still watching me. It was a good feeling.

Time moved on. One year I was performing at Ventura Community College in California. When the performance ended, and people were leaving, I saw one tall person moving down the aisle toward the stage I had just exited. I waited and watched and soon could see that it was Jack Wheeler, Joe's little brother. He had read in the paper that I was to be there, and he had come and brought a friend with him.

What I learned was that Jack had also ended up doing Social Work and was a caseworker with children's issues in the court system. After that visit, every time I was anywhere on that part of the California coast, Jack somehow found out and showed up. His only report on Joe that day was, "He's still in Atlanta."

It was Thanksgiving the following year. I had been out on the road for several weeks and got home to a big pile of mail to open and work my way through. It was mostly bills, as usual, but near the bottom was a letter-looking envelope. In the return address corner was the word "Wheeler" and an Atlanta return address. I tore into the letter quickly. It was from Joe's brother, Jack.

"Dear Donald," it started, "This is from Jack. I am writing to tell you that my brother, Joe, is dying. He has AIDS. He has now gotten to the stage where, with lesions in his brain, he can no longer communicate with anyone. His orders to me were that, when he got to this stage, I was then to write to certain people on a list he made for me and tell them his news...." and there was a little bit more of general politeness before he signed off with his name and an Atlanta telephone number.

I headed straight for the phone and dialed the number.

When Jack answered, I started right in, "Jack ... it's Donald. Why didn't you let me know sooner so I could come to see him?"

Jack's answer was calm and well-worn, "It was part of Joe's plan. He knew that people had a lot of different feelings and prejudices about AIDS, and he didn't want to force any of his friends to try to come to see him and try to say things that maybe made them uncomfortable, maybe they didn't really believe."

Even in his dying, Joe took care of us.

We talked a little bit more, and then I asked, "How's Mama Ruth?"

"She's right here."

Ruth picked up the phone from Jack and, again, I started talking. "It must be pretty bad, Ruth ... you are already there?"

She wasted no words on me: "Don't you remember anything? We are a family who knows how to vote." Then I listened and remembered that dear time in the backyard when she had explained it to me, "Happy or Sad, Rich or Poor, Sick or Well, Live or Die...." You vote each day, and then that day turns out the way you decided it could be."

Ruth went on: "As soon as we learned that Joe was sick, I took my retirement from Baker Furniture, Jack took a leave from his job, Maxine took early retirement, and Guinn came too. We all came down here and moved in with Joe so that every day we could vote for him to live as long as possible. It has been the right thing for all of us to do." We said goodbye.

It was only about two weeks later when Jack called me. Joe had died, and I knew now that I had lost a dear and important friend for good. Or so I thought....

A couple of weeks after the memorial service, a small package arrived in the mail. I could see that it was from Jack, but I had no idea what it could be. I had forgotten about all the carved animals Joe had collected through the years to create his gigantic Noah's Ark collection. With his illness and death, all these animals had ended up with Jack. But, instead of keeping them, Jack had taken that same list of people Joe had instructed him to write and was in the process of sending one of Joe's animals to each of them so that we, his friends, could have to keep something Joe had touched and loved to keep his memory alive with all of us.

So, on that day, I opened the package and unwrapped the small carved animal Jack had sent, but one I was sure that Joe's spirit had chosen just for me, carved to balance on its front hooves with its back feet in the air, a small wooden jackass! And in the box with it, Joe's business card, showing me that when he died, he was a vice-president of The Trust Company

Bank.

I took that little card and turned it over on my desk. Then, on the back side, I wrote four pairs of words: Happy or Sad, Rich or Poor, Sick or Well, Live or Die. It is better than a Monopoly "Get out of Jail Free" card. I forget about it for long periods of time, and then, just when I need it most, I seem to find it again. Then I remember to vote and am once again amazed that we live in a creation in which someone who is no longer alive still has the power to give life to the rest of us.

Chapter Sixteen

Miss Morton

WHEN I MOVED TO CHEROKEE COUNTY, it was 1973. There was no UPS and no 911. Everyone who did not get their mail at the post office had the same address: Route One. This began to be problematic when it came to finding people whom I needed to visit for one reason or another.

The very day I got to town, a church member died. When I asked, "How do I get to Miss Connie's house?" this was the answer I got, several times in slightly differing versions: "You go up there to where the Swans used to live (all the Swans were dead and, I had no idea where they lived when they were alive). Then you turn to the right. Go up that road to where they cut that great big oak tree...." I remained totally lost.

One of the first people I met when I got to town was Mr. John Christy. I knew Mr. Christy's son, who was also a Methodist minister, and I knew his grandchildren from Conference youth work. When I met Mr. Christy, he was seventy-eight years old and his wife, Mary Willie, had recently died.

Mr. Christy was a figure of gigantic proportions in the town of Andrews. He had been the president of the power company, the school board chairman, the master of the lodge, the mayor, and, most importantly, the church treasurer for fifty years. Everyone knew, respected, and trusted Mr. Christy.

Every Monday morning, he would come to the church office where he had a small desk pushed against the side wall. He would enter the deposits from the previous week, pay off the bills that were due, and keep meticulous records of all his church work. It was like having a volunteer business manager for the church.

The following Monday, I approached Mr. Christy with a proposition: "Mr. Christy ..." I started shyly, "I am already having a hard time finding where people live. You know that everyone in town gets their mail at the post office, and there are no street addresses, then out in the country, it is all 'Route One.' Do you think you could make me a list of the people I am likely to need to see the most often and then take me around to show me where they live?"

He agreed. "I know just the kind of list you need," he grinned at me. "I'll think it over and let you know when we can start."

The very next day, he came into the office. "Here you are, preacher. These are the likely ones. I didn't put anyone on this list who is under eighty years old. Most of them live by themselves, and the majority of them are widows.

"Here's what I think: how about if I pick you up after lunch, and we go out each afternoon and meet two people on the list? I'll take you around so that you get introduced to them and maybe tell you a little bit about them. Then the next day, we can go find the next two on the list."

He then handed me the list. It was on a lined sheet of notebook paper, and there were twenty-seven names on it. A few of them were couples, a small number were older men, but the majority were Mrs. Something-or-Another.

The following day we started on our adventures. Mr. Christy picked me up in his green Chevrolet, and we headed out of town. We went to visit Mr. and Mrs. Bristol. Mrs. Bristol had once been the high school Latin teacher, and her husband had worked a small farm. They were one of the few couples on the list.

Then we traveled to see Mrs. Tatham and her daughter. They actually looked about the same age to me. The unnamed daughter had never married, and she and her mother lived in a tiny, faded frame house that, even in the hot summertime, was made hotter by a fire in the front room wood stove.

After this second visit, we headed back toward town. When we got almost to the edge of town, we passed the end of a small, nearly hidden, unpaved road. As we passed this road, Mr. Christy nodded in its direction and said to me, "Up there's where Miss Morton lives."

As the days went on, each weekday afternoon, we visited two more elderly church members. I was learning my way around as Mr. Christy would point out to me where other people lived and sites I needed to know as we made our way. I was gradually marking names off the list.

One thing, though, happened over and over almost every day. Whenever we came back into town from the east side, which was much of the time, we would pass that same little unpaved road. Each time we passed it, Mr. Christy, as if for the very first time, would nod in the direction of the road and repeat, "Up there's where Miss Morton lives," underlining the information more and more each time.

After nearly three weeks, we had visited twenty-six of the twenty-seven places on the list, and I was becoming pretty familiar with the eastern end of Cherokee County. The only name remaining on the list was, to be sure, Miss Morton.

When Mr. Christy let me out at home that afternoon, he gave me the list to keep and announced, "Well, preacher, we're finished!" I knew then that I was to have no personal introduction to Miss Morton. If Mr. Christy would not take me up there, I would have to go there on my own.

Besides Mr. Christy's unspoken warnings, I was picking up various hints around town that Miss Morton was someone to seriously watch out for. I would be walking down the street through town or picking up the mail at the post office when a church member stopped me to inquire: "Have you met *her* yet?" They didn't even use her name as they seemed to know that I would by now have discovered about whom they were talking.

So, finally, the day came when I decided it was time for me to go up that little road and discover Miss Morton.

I jumped in the car and headed up to meet her. I drove to the little road that Mr. Christy had pointed out to me on those many occasions. I remembered where it was, but I had not looked very closely all those times we had passed by. Now, just as I turned into the little dirt road, I had to quickly slam on the brakes. About twenty feet into the road, a fence crossed it. The car could go no farther. It was not a fence with a gate for the road; no, it was a fence with two posts right in the road itself so that there was going to be no driving beyond that point.

Once out of the car, I saw that there was a little V-shaped cow-gap where a sort of trail passed through the fence and continued up what had once been the right-hand side of the now grown-over road. Cautiously, I headed up this little worn trail. About twenty-five yards from the car, I began to hear a big bass-voiced dog starting to bark. At that time in my life, I had never had a dog and was quite afraid of them. As I went on, the barking grew louder, and I kept trying to calculate whether I was closer to the dog or closer to being able to beat it back to the car. The barking continued but did not seem to get any closer.

After maybe fifty more yards, the trail broke out into what would have been a clearing had it not been left to grow back up for many years. Grass, weeds, and wild-looking flowers grew in a jumble about waist-high. And ... there was the dog. It was an ancient mongrelly-looking dog sitting in an old tractor tire on the ground. I quickly realized that the dog was blind and probably even deaf. It knew someone was coming from somewhere, but it couldn't figure out where. It was barking in the wrong direction with its back toward me.

There, on the other side of the grown-over clearing, was the house. It was a frame clapboard, probably painted white when it was built, but obviously not painted since that one early coating.

There was a porch across the front of the house, and the tin roof of the house extended out across the porch. The wooden piers that once supported the front of the porch itself had long ago rotted out. The porch, while still attached to the house, now sloped down to the ground, and the tin roof almost closed down over it. There was no way to get to the front door or for that door to even begin to open.

The chimney at the end of the house had, at one time, followed the outside wall up to the peak of the roof, but, in the intervening years, the chimney and the house had had some sort of falling out. The chimney was still joined to the house at ground level, but they began to separate on the way up until the gap between the chimney and the house was so wide at the top you wondered how it could still stand without seriously violating the laws of common gravity.

The little trail I was following led around to the right-hand end of the house, where a three-step cinderblock stair went up to a door. I headed around to that door and was just about to knock when it opened. There she stood ... Miss Morton!

She looked down at me, standing there on the ground, and proclaimed, "You must be that new little preacher boy. I know everyone else around here, and I don't know you, so you must be the one." From then on, I was, with her, "Preacher Boy."

Since she was standing in the doorway three steps above where I was, my view of her started from the floor up. She was wearing what had to be an oversized pair of men's work brogans. They had no laces, and the tongues flopped down over the toes of the shoes. When she moved her feet, the feet moved first, and then the shoes followed. Her feet had to be rattling around inside the oversized shoes.

She was wearing an old pair of men's Blue Bell-brand bib overalls. One of the braces had given up and was hanging loose while the overalls were being supported by the survivor. Under the overalls, she had on an old olive drab Army surplus wool shirt. The shirt still had someone's sergeant stripes sewn on the sleeve and the name "Brookbank" sewn on over the shirt pocket.

Then I came to her face. It was a playground of wrinkles that ran to and fro, right and left, leaving no flat skin undisturbed. Her blue eyes studied me through rimless glasses.

Finally, there was her hair. It looked like it might have been swept up off the floor of the Brillo factory on Friday afternoon, then got wet on Saturday and rusted.

"Come on in," she offered, "So I can look at you."

I climbed the three steps and entered the house into what was literally the "living room" since it was obviously where she lived.

There was a wood stove in the far corner of the room with the stovepipe running out through the wall. This was on the opposite end of the house from the leaning chimney, which had not seen service for some time.

There were two cane-bottom chairs in the room, one serving as a desk chair for a small table that doubled as a desk.

Then there was the bed. The bed was actually an old sleeper sofa upholstered in green vinyl. It was not the kind with a mattress that unfolds from within its frame. No, it was the old kind with a back that simply flopped down flat, and then the back and the seat together made the sleeping surface.

The back was permanently down, and on the sleeper was her Army surplus mummy-style wool sleeping bag snugged up against two feather pillows at one arm of the sofa bed.

On the floor beside the bed were her accouterments of the night. A worn, blue-bound bible with an Eastern Star emblem on the front lay near two small water glasses with some water still in them. I saw an open green jar of Vaseline petroleum jelly, a lidded jar of Vicks VapoRub, a box of Kleenex, and a little pile of high-mileage Q-tips.

She sat down on the bed and motioned for me to sit down beside her. We then began to get acquainted as she told me her version of her life story.

She was the child, she said, of "Faith Missionary parents." She had gone to a teachers' college and had spent forty years as a high school English teacher. She told me, "I taught English at every high school in seven counties in this part of North Carolina." I later got out the map and added up all the high schools in these seven counties and realized that she must have been "highly recommended" very frequently.

About that time, she announced, "It's about time to eat dinner ... let's go in the kitchen and we'll get something to eat." There was no question about this; it was simply a declarative announcement. "Be careful as you go in there. It's where I keep my rock collection."

We went out of the front room into the small kitchen on one side of the house, and sure enough, it was where she kept her rock collection. Rows of neatly organized rocks covered the entire floor except for a narrow path leading to the refrigerator and sink. The kitchen table was totally covered with neat rows of rocks. The kitchen counters were covered with neat rows of rocks. The doors had been removed from the old wooden kitchen cabinets, and they were totally filled with neat rows of rocks. There were rocks in the sink that had not yet been washed and put into neat rows. "This is quite a rock collection," was my only comment.

She led me over to the small refrigerator and pulled open the door. Inside the refrigerator, there were only two things: Reese's Peanut Butter Cups and small, green glass bottles of Coca-Cola.

She reached in with one hand and pulled out a Peanut Butter Cup while with the other hand, she pulled a pocketknife out of her overall pocket. Opening the pocketknife, she carefully cut the candy in half and handed one half to me while she held on to the other for herself. Then, much to my relief, we each got our own Coca-Cola.

We returned to the sofa, where she had me ask the blessing, and then we had dinner together.

After that, I thought it was time for me to go, but she was not yet ready for my departure. "You can't go until you see my cats."

"Oh," I responded, "I saw them out in the yard when I got here." I thought that would take care of it.

"Oh, no!" She came back at me. "You only saw the yellow ones ... I let them out by the color ... I can keep up with them better that way. Come on back here, and you can see the rest of them."

She led me back to a little hallway that paralleled the kitchen. She showed me three doors in a row on the right side of the hallway. I could see, strangely, that the top panel of each door had been sawed off just above its top hinges. Locating a three-step kitchen stool in the hallway, Miss Morton pulled the stool over to the first door and instructed me to step up and look over the top. "This room is for black and white cats, black or white, or any combination of those two colors of cats." I looked over the sawed-off door, and sure enough, there were about a dozen cats in the otherwise empty room, all of which were dominated by black and/or white coloring.

"This middle room is for the yellow cats. It's a little bigger because I always seem to have more of them. They're all outside right now, so there's nobody in there to look at. This back room is the smallest one, and it's reserved for the miscellany."

I stepped up onto the stool and looked over this last door. The few cats in this last room were various blends of calico, brindle—and one that, for all the world, was on the edge of red.

"How many do you have?" I cautiously asked.

"This morning, or right now?" she asked. Then, without waiting for my answer, she continued, "This morning I had an even thirty, but I seem to have picked up two more yellow tigers since then." I was in the process of discovering that the little stub of a road where I had parked had become the dropping-off place for unwanted cats in the eastern end of Cherokee

County.

I praised the cats, thanked Miss Morton for our meal, and said my goodbyes. I had just made the first of an uncountable number of visits I would make to the little house over the next half-dozen years.

Gradually, in spite of my own shyness or fear, I came to deeply appreciate and dearly enjoy that old lady. As time passed, there would be moments when, down in town, I would get my fill of "normal." Whenever those times came, all I needed to do was to head up for an afternoon at Miss Morton's house to have my sense of the world's uniqueness restored.

As time went on, Gerald and Nancy Bunyan moved to nearby Robbinsville, and they joined the church in Andrews. Gerald had had a career as the zoo veterinarian at the Cleveland, Ohio, zoo, and they had retired to a lovely home on Lake Santeetlah just over the ridge from where we lived.

It had been Gerald's intention to totally retire from veterinary medicine with this move. He and Nancy had some acreage around their house, and his plan was to garden, read, and be retired.

One day Gerald went over to a neighbor's house to borrow a tiller he had been offered so he could work up a patch of land he planned to turn into an asparagus patch. When he arrived at the neighbor's house, the man's wife redirected him, "He's down at the barn. There's trouble with one of the cows."

When Gerald arrived at the barn, he found his distraught neighbor fretting over one of his best cows who was down in her stall. Gerald told me later that, after a brief conversation with the neighbor, he knew exactly what the trouble was. The cow was trying to birth a dead calf.

Gerald went on to ask me, "What was I going to do? Was I going to just stand there and watch the man's cow die, or was I going to 'come out?'" He came out.

Explaining to the farmer what he really was, he took the man's old Case pocketknife, sterilized it with a Zippo cigarette lighter, and went into the cow, dissected the dead calf, and took it out a piece at a time. The cow lived, and, as the word spread, the following day, Gerald was back in the veterinary business!

He did not open an office. No, he just equipped a Dodge pickup truck and made both house and farm calls. People loved him! There was no one within about seventy-five miles who did large animal work, and this was what Gerald loved the most. "Compared to a Water Buffalo, I'll take a Hereford bull any day," he once told me.

It was not long after that when Gerald came over one day to see me. "I've heard about this lady with all the cats," he started. "Miss Morton? That's not a very safe situation with regard to rabies, especially with all the raccoons around this part of the world. I'd like to go up there and offer to vaccinate them for her, and everyone tells me that you are the right person to take me up there."

I was happy to do so, and, with a warning that he should not expect to get paid, the following afternoon we made our way up to Miss Morton's house.

She didn't hear us coming until I knocked on the door. When she answered, she looked suspiciously at Dr. Bunyan as if he was someone she had never seen, and she wondered what he was doing there. I took over, "Miss Morton, this is Dr. Bunyan."

"I'm not sick ... what's he doing here?"

"No," I was quick to insert. "He's not a human doctor. He's a cat doctor."

She just about laughed her head off at that.

Dr. Bunyan now took over, "I've heard that you have a lot of very nice cats. Donald's told me about them. I asked him to bring me up here so I could meet you and see your cats. And while we are here, I would really like to vaccinate them against rabies. You know that there are a lot of raccoons around here, and they are bad to carry rabies."

"I didn't ask you to come up here, and I'm not going to pay for something that I didn't ask for." It was not a mean reply, just a simple matter of fact to her.

"Oh, no," Gerald went on. "I didn't come asking to get paid, I just came asking to vaccinate them as a community service. It's good for the community for the cats to be safe from rabies for everyone's sake."

She finally decided that it would be okay, and we started the vaccination project.

Gerald was in absolutely no hurry. He sat on the sleeper sofa, and she brought him the first cat. "Now, what is his name?" Gerald started, "It's not right to give a shot to a cat that you haven't properly met."

"This is Oscar," she almost smiled at her pleasure in the way he was treating her cats.

Every time she handed him a new cat, he learned its name and loved on it until the cat in hand was purring under his gentle care. When he gave them the shot, they never even stopped purring. They didn't even know when it happened. None of them even wanted to get out of his lap when it was time for the next one to get its turn.

There was one old cat named "Captain." He was spending his time in a box under the wood stove in the living room. He was profoundly old and had almost no hair. His body was covered with lumps and sores. Gerald handled him very carefully and held him for quite a long time.

He was still holding Captain when he asked Miss Morton a straightforward question: "Miss Morton, you know that Captain is not a well cat. He has cancer, and his tumors are multiplying. He really is in misery. Would you like for me to help Captain go on his peaceful way to cat heaven?"

She had watched the caring way he had loved on her old cat with tears in her eyes. By now, she was convinced that he loved all the cats as much as she did. She wept as she answered, "For his benefit, I think that would be an acceptable and wonderful thing." She then held Captain while Dr. Bunyan gently put him to sleep. Gerald and I even dug the grave and had a little graveside service under her direction before we left that day.

Just as we were ready to depart, she looked at us and announced, "You've done such a good job that I've decided to pay you, Doctor." Without waiting for a response, she disappeared into the kitchen. When she returned, she counted out to him, in dimes, three dollars and ten cents. That was ten cents per cat for vaccinating thirty-one cats on that day.

After that, Gerald Bunyan made regular visits with me so that the cats were always up to date with rabies and other needed vaccinations. They were probably the overall healthiest cats in Cherokee County.

One day, I went up to her house, and when she opened the door, she was wearing a homemade bandage tied under her chin and knotted over the top of her head. She looked like Marley's ghost in an old black-and-white version of *A Christmas Carol*. Her jaw was obviously swollen, and there was a strong smell of Vicks in the air.

"What in the world is the matter with your jaw?" I immediately asked.

"I've got an abscessed tooth, and it's coming through to the outside," she pulled the bandage aside so I could see what

I did not want to see.

"You've got to go to the dentist and get that tooth out," I was not being polite; this simply had to be done.

She replied, "I've been downtown to that dentist, and I am not going back." She explained, "He took one look at me and told me that he would have to put me to sleep! I jumped out of that chair and ran all the way back home. I remembered old Captain, and I was not about to have that done to me!"

After that declaration, it seemed to be up to me to figure out the solution. I began going from dentist to dentist throughout what seemed like all of Western North Carolina, trying to explain her and the situation she was in. They just shook their heads.

At last, I found a dentist in Bryson City who agreed to give it a try. I took her over there, and he spent the entire afternoon wiggling that old molar and finally splitting it into two halves until he eventually worried it out. He told me when he finished, "I was scared to death I was going to break her jaw. She is so frail."

I thought, *she's a lot tougher than she looks.*

With the tooth out and a good ten days of antibiotics, she was almost back to ... I almost thought, "normal!"

One afternoon Gerald Bunyan and I went up to see Mrs. Morton. He wanted to take her some sweet potatoes from his garden and, at the same time, make sure there were not some new vaccination candidates he had not yet tended to.

When she came to the door, he offered, "Miss Morton... I just dug my sweet potatoes." Holding out a brown paper bag, he announced, "I brought you some."

Instead of reaching for the offered gift, she inquired, "Are they cooked?" The potatoes went back home with Dr. Bunyan.

We vaccinated a couple of new cats before leaving, and then she asked him. "Dr. Bunyan ... you know that I am getting kind of old, and I seem to get more and more cats. Besides what people drop off, the rest of them seem to be causing more on their own. I just had that little litter of four black ones you said are still too little to get their shots. Is there some way you can put the tomcats in neutral and slow down their reproduction?"

I think Gerald had been waiting for this topic to come up, but he was cautious about being the one to raise it. "Let me go down to the truck and get some supplies. Then if you catch them one at a time, I can throw them out of gear."

He headed down the trail to the Dodge pickup that was his office and returned with only two items: he had a scalpel and one large rubber boot.

Gerald sat down on the chopping block stump in the side yard and positioned the boot between his knees. He had the scalpel in his right hand. "Okay ... I'm ready. Bring me the first one."

She caught and then brought to him a large orange cat whom she called Apricot. Gerald took the big cat into his arms, cuddled it, scratched it under the chin, and rubbed its belly until it was in full-volume purr. Then, in what seemed like a half-second skilled maneuver, he suddenly dropped the cat head-first into the boot, clamped his hind legs together so that it could not move, lifted its tail, and went "swish" with the scalpel, the cat was released and it ran off into the edge of the woods licking its new wound but having no real idea what had just happened to it.

"We don't teach it like that in veterinary school," he commented. "But if you do it the whole long way, you might lose one or more out of a hundred to the anesthesia. I never lost a cat doing it like this, and they're over it in no time." That afternoon we put seventeen tomcats in neutral, and Miss Morton was very happy indeed.

Every year, down at the church, we had a large fir tree put up in the sanctuary a few weeks before Christmas. The tree had a few Christmas symbol decorations, but mostly it was known as the White Gift Tree.

People would purchase presents for unknown recipients, wrap them in plain white paper, and place them under the tree. The wrapped gifts bore simple labels like: "for six-year-old boy," "for size 10 girl," "toy for elementary age girl," etc. After the Christmas Eve service, the presents would be gathered and given to Joe Wheeler, who was then working for Social Services, and Joe would see that they were taken to homes to which Santa Claus had lost his map.

In addition to the gifts placed under the tree, there was a bag of clothespins nearby. People would take a clothespin and pin currency to the limbs of the tree. There were a lot of dollar bills pinned by children whose parents gave them the dollar, but there were also fives, tens, and an occasional twenty. Following the Christmas Eve service, a committee from the church would meet and divide the money up, and it would be taken the next day to homes where a small bit of cash would make a large difference.

Following the first Christmas Eve service when I was there, I remember well that committee meeting where the currency was counted and divided. Immediately, someone volunteered to take some of the cash to the Roper's house. There was a willing volunteer to take the designated amount to the Wooten's. In fact, there were volunteers all around until we came to Miss Morton's name. Without any discussion at all, the committee voiced in unison, "The preacher will do it!" By this time, I knew her well enough that I was happy to go.

That night, December twenty-fourth, was the only true Christmas Eve snowfall I remember in my life. It snowed all night, and the next morning, the world was silent and beautiful. It was also my assignment to take the Christmas money to Miss Morton. It was almost midday by the time we had dealt with Christmas morning as a family, and there was a bit of time to make the delivery before our own big meal.

I got in the car and carefully drove through the quiet snow up to Miss Morton's.

She did not hear me coming until I knocked on the door. She opened it with great surprise. "What are you doing here, Preacher Boy? It's Christmas!"

"Oh," I smiled, "I just came up to bring you something from the church for Christmas. Can I come in the house?" She invited me into the living room, which was overheated to the point of discomfort by the wood stove in the corner.

"You brought me something? What is it?"

I handed her a plain paper envelope. "I think it's some money for Christmas," I answered shyly.

"How much is it?" she held onto the envelope.

"I don't know ... you'll have to count it." She opened the envelope and counted out twenty-seven one-dollar bills. I shall never forget what happened next. She carefully counted the money over again, then seemed to go into another world as she worked through things in her head. Then she counted out four of the dollar bills, folded them, and put them into the pocket of her usual bib overalls. Then she placed the rest of the money back into the envelope and handed it back to me.

"Take this back down to the church and use it for someone in need." The conversation was finished.

That week, between Christmas and New Year's, we were having the last meeting of the year to set the final church budget for the coming year. Up until that point, I had thought of all kinds of reasons I hoped that the church would raise my salary ... until she pulled that little trick! After that, I could not ask for a penny more than what I was already making. I had discovered the personal meaning of that great gap that exists between "need" and "want."

I was no longer in Andrews when the end of life came for Miss Morton. No, after five years, I was sent on to another United Methodist appointment in Charlotte, North Carolina. But I kept up with people in Andrews and, in parts and pieces, heard reports of the down-flow of her life.

The preacher who came after me never got to know her, and that was sad to me. She added spice and flavor to all of my life.

Gradually, I heard that she developed diabetes (probably had the condition for a while before it was diagnosed). She called it "the sugar." As time went on, she lost a leg to the sugar and had to be sent (against her will, I am sure) to a care facility in northwest Georgia, where she lived out her life.

The favorite story I heard, however, was wonderful and did not surprise me at all.

When she had to leave her home, she let it be known that she needed to see Dr. Bunyan. When he arrived, she handed him a cigar box and told him that his instructions were in the box, and he was to follow them to the letter. When he opened the box, he found thirty-four one-dollar bills and a handwritten letter from her. She told him that he was to use the thirty-four dollars as pay to put her remaining thirty-four cats to sleep and have them cremated so that they could be buried with her when she died, as she was sure no one else would love and care for them the way she did.

Gerald laughed, "You can forget that." He went on, "I've got too much money in those cats." He ended up taking all of them home with him. As his wife, Nancy, told the story, every child who came within cat-tossing distance for the next couple of months went home with a well-vaccinated cat!

When I think about my time with Miss Morton and the many things I learned from her, it is difficult to put them all in order. Finally, though, I have boiled all those learnings down to three things:

First of all, never in all of my life will I ever be so poor that I cannot still honestly call myself wealthy.

Secondly, it is so very important to have people like Miss Morton living on the fringes of our communities. They are the ones who allow the rest of us to live with the delicious illusion that we are normal!

Lastly, if you want to live forever, be weird! To this day, when I return to Andrews, I still hear people, more than fifty years later, telling stories about her.

Chapter Seventeen

Otto and Marguerite

I FIRST MET OTTO AND MARGUERITE WOOD when Otto was seventy-five years old, and Marguerite was—she cupped her hands around her mouth and whispered as she told me, as if no one else could hear her—"seventy-six."

It was 1973, and I had just moved far back into the Cherokee County corner of the North Carolina mountains, even farther back than Haywood County, where I had grown up. I was there to be the Director of the county-wide United Methodist Parish, and I soon met Otto and Marguerite as the musicians for the Saturday night community folk and square dances at the John C. Campbell Folk School in Brasstown, North Carolina, on the edge of Cherokee County.

You could not meet Otto and Marguerite even briefly without immediately being pulled into the charm of their in-credible energy for living. They were two people who simply bubbled over with joy in every waking moment and in everything in which they were involved.

The Woods were both physically tiny people. Otto was short and, except for a white decorative fringe as a frame, completely bald. He was the fiddle player, but he was so small that, when he pulled out his fiddle, many people thought it was a viola.

Marguerite was even smaller. A tiny bird-like creature, she seemed to trip along with her feet hardly touching the ground. She was the piano player, floating above the piano bench, bent over the keyboard, and always smiling, showing all of her teeth. She played gigantic chords all over the piano to undergird and drive Otto's melodies.

The Woods quickly and easily became the kind of friends you feel you have known all your life, and I soon found myself consumed by their whole life story.

Both Otto and Marguerite (he called her "Marge" when they talked, but no one else was allowed that intimacy) were born in Grand Rapids, Michigan, in 1897 and 1898. As Otto told his own story, he and his brother "had the first full-service gasoline station ever opened in the city of Grand Rapids." He was never quite sure of the date but was quite certain that they were in business before 1920.

As a child, Otto had taken classical violin lessons, and the combination of his musical acumen and his mechanical skill continued throughout his life.

Marguerite's first job was "running the cash register at

the dime store." She, though, had had early piano lessons, and when the two of them met, it was music that was the center and the very love of their shared life.

Otto once told me that he had played for his first dance when he was sixteen years old, but that he didn't get to play for the entire dance. He had to leave early because his mother had ordered that he be home by ten o'clock!

Otto and Marguerite got married in their mid-twenties, and as it turned out, they never had any children. Otto was the one who told me about that. "It just didn't happen," he said. "Of course, that meant that we had more time to think about things. Without children to take care of, by the time we were in our forties, we had life pretty much figured out."

I wanted to hear more about that, and when I asked, neither one was shy to explain: "We began to notice," he went on, "that people around us spent their lives in one of two ways. Some of them *bought* things, and some of them *did* things."

At this point, Marguerite broke in (they were always finishing one another's sentences). "And when people buy things," she chuckled, "then they have to take care of them."

Otto picked up her unfinished sentence. "... and that's worse than just having children to begin with."

The end of this philosophical discussion was that, with no children to whom anything might be left, in their early forties, Otto and Marguerite decided to spend the rest of their lives "doing things."

They had made it through the Depression, and now the post-war economy was picking up. People needed recreational activities wherever they lived. So, Otto sold his half of the gasoline station to his brother. Marguerite quit her job at the dime store, and they became "traveling musicians for life," playing music that pulled the dance out of the feet of everyone who heard it.

At one time, Otto had a small, on-the-side dance band. He even showed me a piece of letterhead once that said, "Otto Dale Wood and his Orchestra." But now it was to be just the two of them, a streamlined family operation, designed so that they could be free to come, go, travel, play music, and, in their own words, "do things."

Some of Marguerite's relatives owned a resort hotel she described as being "on the shores of Lake Michigan." (She never told me exactly *where.*) With that connection, she and Otto began to play music for the summer guests' listening and dancing. As wartime came to an end, business there boomed, and they were enlisted not only as musicians but also to change beds and clean rooms. She said, "When you're working for rich relatives, and you are the poor connection, then you have to do whatever they tell you."

Their playing at this hotel soon led to other jobs nearby, and soon, the Woods were playing a full schedule at a series of resorts up and down the eastern shoreline of the lake.

At about this time, Otto also began more actively calling dances, especially singing squares. As a teenager, he had often played dances at what he referred to as "the USOs or whatever they called those soldiers' clubs" of the First World War. It was there, he said, that he absorbed the singing square dances that he would later call "American Singing Squares." When questioned, he had no specific memory of whom he had heard as the callers or when he had first heard certain dances called. "I was just playing the fiddle," he said, "Not paying attention. But it happened so much that it sort of soaked into me, and later when people were just standing around listening to the music, I remembered those calls and got people to do them again." (Once in a while at the Folk School, Otto would introduce a dance by saying, "I've been calling this particular dance for more than fifty years.")

By the time Otto was telling me this, he was nearing eighty, and he had his own personal memories all worked out. This is the way he had processed the memory:

"Those dance callers in the soldiers' clubs had microphones that would amplify their voices. This was a new thing, a thing they had never had before, that they could talk and be heard even while the music was playing. I think that's why I remembered those calls. They were just calls that soaked into your head because you already had the tune living up there."

Here's one of the first ones I remember.... The tune is "The Red River Valley."

Oh, the first couple lead down the valley,
Where you circle to the left and to the right,
Then you swing that girl in the valley,
Now you swing with your own Red River gal.

The call went on and on until it had repeated enough for all the couples to lead the dance and everyone to end up back in their "home" place where they started.

Otto's list of old dances went on and on. There was "I Want a Girl," "Hinky-Dinky-Parlez-Vous," "McNamara's Band," "Oh Johnny Oh," "Solomon Levi," "You Call Everybody Darling" ... the list seemed to be endless. Otto remembered more and more the longer he talked.

Once Otto started calling, he kept adding more dances to later popular tunes, some of which are identifiable in terms of later well-known callers who composed them, some of which he may have devised himself, and many of which are of vague and unknown origin, except that many people for years associated them only with him. These "Otto Wood Dances" were to such tunes as "Too Old to Cut the Mustard," "Louisiana Swing," "O Lonesome Me," "Take Me Back to Tulsa," and Pancho Baird's "Smoke on the Water."

The only problem with playing at the Lake Michigan hotels was that business there was seasonal, and, when summer was over, so was their employment.

Ever resourceful, however, and always outgoing, Otto and Marguerite had met several summer residents who were spending their winters on the newly developing Gulf Coast of Florida. Soon it was suggested that they come to the Sunshine State to play music for the winter season.

Very quickly, they developed a two-part year-round rhythm to their lives, which was to last for some time and provide stability to their music and dance careers: Lake Michigan in the summer, the Gulf Coast of Florida in the winter.

Now that World War Two was over, it was the right time to go to Florida. Otto and Marguerite bought a small trailer in Palmetto, Florida, near Bradenton. This was to be their winter home and work base until the end of their lives.

Marguerite used to love to tell stories about the trips from Michigan to Florida. They had an old Ford car in those days, and nearly all their possessions made the trip with them to Florida and back each year.

Otto drove the car. The rest of the front seat, floor to ceiling, was piled with all the things they "might need" during the winter months. Marguerite rode in the back seat, directly behind Otto, and the rest of the back seat was as filled as the front. We never learned what had filled the Ford's trunk to begin with.

As she started the story, I had to ask the question: "Why did you ride back there in the back by yourself instead of up in the front with Otto?"

"It was safe," she smiled. "No matter what I did or said back there, he couldn't reach me!"

Marguerite went on to explain that the Ford had no radio, but that she had packed all of her musical instruments on top in the back seat so that she could "play music for Otto to drive by." There were several wooden recorders, her Wheatstone English concertina, and her accordion. On the very top of the pile was her little two-and-a-half octave harpsichord, the lid fastened down and the legs removed so it would ride there. She could reach them all, even the keys of the harpsichord.

"It made the trip go faster," she explained. "You see, it was two-lane roads all the way from Michigan to Florida back then. As soon as I started playing something that Otto didn't like, we got there a whole lot faster."

One of her favorite recollections was the story of one particular trip when she decided to play "music by Mister Mozart." Everything was fine until she got to *Don Giovanni*. Otto hated the music, and, the more Marguerite played, the faster he drove. It was *Don Giovanni* on the recorder, then the same thing on the concertina. Next came *Don Giovanni* on the harpsichord and finally a reprise on the accordion. Otto was headed at full speed for Palmetto!

"We came to a place called 'Starke,'" Marguerite reported, "and another sound joined Mister Mozart." It was the siren of a Starke police car that, with red light flashing, pulled Otto to the side of the road.

Furious, Otto was out of the car and verbally engaged with the policeman in a flash. All the anger he had built up for

Marguerite came pouring out of his mouth toward the officer of the law who had been unfortunate enough to stop him. The policeman, who was, Marguerite recalled, "two feet taller than Otto," responded by patting Otto on the top of his bald head and warning, "You'd better cool down, little feller!"

Then Marguerite's story went on, "Otto used words ... Well ... I don't know where he learned those words!"

That's when the policeman decided that Otto needed to meet the magistrate. The magistrate decided that Mister Otto Wood should go to jail for one hour, "until his vocabulary and manners both improved." So, Otto was locked up in the jail to spend his hour with the drunks left over from the night before.

I asked Marguerite, "What did you do while Otto was in jail for the hour?"

"Oh," she laughed out loud now, "I just parked the Ford under a tree outside the jail, rolled down the windows, and played Mister Mozart so that the prisoners could have some nice music to listen to."

The Woods both remembered that it was 1946 when Frank Smith invited them to be musicians for a dance week at Berea College in Kentucky. There they met and fell in love with the world of Country Dance, a love they would hold to themselves and nourish in others throughout the remaining thirty-five years of their lives.

Not long after that (first-of-many weeks) at Berea, the two

of them were brought to the John C. Campbell Folk School in Brasstown, North Carolina, to play for a summer dance course there. The Danish-patterned Folk School had been a center for both Danish and English Country Dance since its founding in 1925, and by the time the Woods first came there in the late 1940s, the dance program was very strong. It was this initial visit to Brasstown that changed their lives and removed them from Michigan forever.

New friends in the Country Dance world and the charm of the North Carolina mountains led the Woods to soon sell their home in Michigan and build a small house on the edge of Brasstown. For the last three decades of their lives, they lived and played music on the Florida Gulf Coast during the winter and in the North Carolina mountains every summer.

The word "thrifty" does not begin to describe the Woods' economic efficiency. They could live more fully and happily on next-to-nothing than most other people managed to live with reasonable access to everything. And they were proud of it!

Again and again, people heard Otto make one of his favorite speeches: "I don't understand why old people complain so much about not having enough money. Why, we have our Social Security to live on ... and last year, we saved more than a thousand dollars out of that!" The general consensus was that they lived on air.

One day, when they were in their late seventies, I went by the Wood's house for a visit. When I got to the little house, they were not at home. As I started to leave, their car, now a Volkswagen Beetle, came rolling up in the driveway. Otto got out on the driver's side of the car and started toward the house. When Marguerite got out on her side, she was holding a small, brown paper bag in her arm.

"Where have you been?" I asked. "I was afraid I had missed you."

"We've been to the store," she answered. "We go to the store about this time every day so we can buy our food for the day. It's best to go grocery shopping when you are not hungry, so you won't overdo things."

"You go every day?" I rejoined. "Wouldn't it be a whole lot easier to go only once or twice a week?"

Marguerite laughed, "Oh, that might be wasteful. At our age, we might die and not get to eat it all."

From early May until mid-October, the Woods played for dances at the Folk School from one to four nights each week. They always played for the Community Dance on Saturday nights. There would be a caller who organized the evening and called the dances, a mixture of English, Danish, and American traditions, depending on who was calling. Otto and Marguerite provided the music for them all. In addition, Otto always called from two to four of his "American Singing Squares" on Saturday evenings. In his lifetime, no one else ever called these particular dances; they were his exclusive territory. The musical arrangements for the singing squares were unique. Only he and Marguerite knew exactly how to make them work.

The Woods also played when classes were held on other nights. There might be one night each week on which a beginners' class was held and another night for more advanced dancers. Sometimes there was a night for rapper sword or longsword dancers or even for garland dancers. Besides the regular classes, there were other occasions when a group of dancers would be pulled together to present programs representing the Folk School. These programs often included a square or two called by Otto.

Scheduled and planned completely apart from these events were full weeks of being staff musicians for dance and music weeks, the Craftsmen's Fair in Asheville (playing there again for Folk School dancers), the Folk School Fall Festival, and other dance weekends.

One year I was involved in helping to work out the pay arrangements for the Woods as musicians for the regular weekly dances. We started by asking them to tell us what they needed in order to play for the Saturday night Community Dance as this was the most important event of the week. Their request was that they be paid ten dollars for playing a two-hour Community Dance on Saturday evenings. This was their total request for both of them, not ten dollars each. Otto and Marguerite wanted ten dollars for them both together.

"That's all we need," they insisted. "You shouldn't have to pay us any more than we need." They refused to ask for any pay for the class nights. "That's when people come to learn," Marguerite insisted, "We shouldn't have to get paid to help people learn."

Our committee decided that their request was simply not enough, so, without asking them, we set the pay at twenty dollars instead of ten for Saturday nights.

Otto and Marguerite responded to this generosity by accepting the ten dollars per week for which they had asked and then using the other ten dollars to establish a fund to purchase a much-needed new piano for the hall, thereby effectively embarrassing everyone else into contributing to the fund.

The Woods were, in reality, extremely talented and near-perfectionists as musicians. Their beginnings were classical, and their expectations of themselves were always higher than anyone else could ask of them. Though the old upright piano that was to be replaced when the new fund reached its goal (which it did in a short time) was terrible, no one had ever heard Marguerite complain about it. One day, when someone seemed to be trying to coax a complaint out of her, she responded, "A *real* piano player *never* complains about the piano. Everyone here knows that the old piano is terrible. The piano player's job is to play it, not try to tell people something they already know."

When the dance being called was Danish, Marguerite often switched to the accordion, and sometimes, when the dance formation was circular, the two of them would play standing in the center of the big ring of dancers, Marguerite on the accordion and Otto on his fiddle.

Both of the Woods were fine recorder players, and Marguerite was also accomplished on the English concertina. She was quite proud that she had earlier acquired and perfectly cared for an old Wheatstone, for her the very Stradivarius of concertinas.

If anyone talked about musical talent, Marguerite responded by referring to herself as a "hack piano player," but there were many memorable occasions that showed clearly that this opinion was her own self-effacement, the voice of her proper Midwestern humility, and not an honest assessment of her talents.

Once, during a summer dance week, the Woods had been joined on the musical staff of the Folk School by Philip Merrill of New York City. A regular in Brasstown at certain seasons of the year, Philip's musical career had ranged from his start as a theatre organist for silent movies to his later long-term position as Music Director for the Country Dance and Song Society of America. All the while, he was called on to serve as an audition accompanist for Broadway show tryouts in the city, Philip also played accordion, recorder, and English concertina.

As the dancers were gathering to sing a few songs between dinner and the evening dance that week, Marguerite announced that she and Philip were going to "play a little something so that people will know we can do more than just bang out dance tunes." They then pulled out their two concertinas and proceeded to play, without music, Bach's "Double Concerto for Two Violins" on English concertinas, leaving everyone in the room speechless.

One summer during Recorder week at the Folk School, there was an unusually large number of student registrations. The instructors for the week were, again, Philip Merrill from New York, plus the author of *The Recorder Book,* Johanna Kulbach herself! There were so many students signed up, though, that Marguerite was recruited to teach an additional beginners' class.

Each evening, the classes would play one another music they had worked on during the day, and the three instructors would present models of performance perfection for everyone's benefit. Marguerite always praised Johanna and Philip and expressed appreciation that they would even let her play with them.

John Ramsay was the director of the Folk School at the time, and, for the closing evening, he presented a little song with words he had written to the tune of "The Irish Washerwoman." His original song expressed the knowledge that the students who had gathered for the week had already figured out. The words went like this:

> *Oh, Johanna is flat and Phil Merrill don't know it,*
> *Phil Merrill is flat and Johanna don't know it,*
> *They're both of them flat, but they sound pretty good,*
> *To everyone else except Marguerite Wood!*

She was the consummate perfectionist!

One year I spent the better part of the winter building a harpsichord. It was a full-sized affair built on a Burton kit I had obtained. When it was finished, I decided it should be inaugurated by Marguerite. When I showed it to her and asked her to be the first person to play it, she blushed. Then she said, "Would twenty-three minutes be too long?" and proceeded to play a Mozart concerto that was exactly twenty-three minutes long, again, with no music.

Although Otto had left the automobile service business when he sold his half of the gasoline station to his brother, he could forever tune cars as perfectly as violins. More than once, I remember someone coming to the Folk School to look for him, having been sent by some local resident when the visitor had car trouble. One day a man arrived in an ancient sputtering Citroen. Otto simply heard the car coming and said, "You know, you really need to set the timing on those things when they are cold ... not after they get warmed up," then he instructed the driver to leave the car at the Wood's house overnight, and it would be "well" in the morning.

Marguerite did have a sharp tongue. She did not hold back on comments or opinions. She "blamed" this talent on her first music teacher, a person whom she described as a "terrible musician who taught me more about music than anyone else with whom I ever studied." To unravel this seeming contradiction, she explained: "She always told me exactly what she thought about my playing.... That's what I learned from ... you must have a heart of pure love to teach like that!" We all knew that Marguerite's often narrow opinions still came from an honest heart of pure love.

As musicians, the Woods had played inseparably for so long that they almost functioned as a single unit. In fact, except for select friends (like Philip Merrill), they did not particularly care to be joined by other musicians. The two of them considered it especially offensive when some other musician, who just happened to be present for a dance, assumed that it was acceptable to sit in and play along without asking their permission.

On one occasion, memorable to many, Otto and Marguerite were playing for the Folk School Fall Festival weekend. A fiddle player, with whom many present were already acquainted, walked into the dance hall, proceeded up to the stage, and commenced to take out his fiddle and join the Woods without asking for their consent.

The dance started, and the chosen tune was "The Devil's Dream," a well-known fiddle tune in the key of A major, a good open-string key for fiddle players. The music started, but something seemed to be wrong. The uninvited "guest" fiddler couldn't find the tune! After trying through a full round of the dance, the same walk-on fiddler put his instrument away and eased out the back door of the dance hall. Otto and Marguerite smiled at one another. They had quickly moved to play "The Devil's Dream" in the improbable fiddle key of A flat!

After Otto's death, when, at Marguerite's suggestion, I began to call some of "Otto's dances," with her at the piano. Marguerite transcribed for me some of the musical arrangements she and Otto had worked out to go with them. Again and again, the tunes would be transcribed, not in their normal keys like G, D, or A, but in very difficult fiddle keys such as E flat, A flat, and D flat. Marguerite smiled when asked about that and replied that those were the keys in which Otto liked to sing the calls. I was fairly certain, however, that moving a normal D major tune into either E flat or D flat had less to do with Otto's singing choice than with preserving the harmonic exclusivity of their musical club.

In the autumn of 1975, we were all preparing for the Fall Festival Weekend at the Folk School. Garnet Sloan was at this time in charge of the Folk School Dance Program, though his official position on the staff was as an instructor in weaving. Garnet had, though, been one of the Berea Country Dancers as a college student and had briefly danced with Martha Graham, and the Folk School Dance Program was his voluntary secondary occupation.

On Friday before the big weekend came, Garnet's father died in Kentucky, and he departed for the funeral, leaving us with no dance caller for this, one of the most important events of the Folk School year.

Fall Festival was not, per se, a dance weekend. It was,

rather, an arts and crafts fair weekend. During the weekend, though, Folk School dancers performed several times, and, in addition, the Saturday night community dance would be much larger than normal with so many extra people there. We knew that there would be no problem with the dance demonstrations, but it seemed to everyone that we would simply have to call off the community dance in Garnet's absence.

Several of us were talking over this problem when, all at once, Otto looked at me and said, "You'll do it!"

"What do you mean, 'I'll do it?'" I asked with shock. "I've never done anything like this in my life."

Otto went on, "We've played for so many of these dances that we know exactly how every one of them goes. Marge and I will make out the program for you ... we'll make it easy because there will be so many visitors here.... I'll be right behind you and tell you exactly what to tell them, so they won't get lost." By Saturday morning, they had handed me a neatly typed plan, complete with directions about formations and exactly how to teach each dance they had planned for the evening. With that, I became an instant dance caller!

Later on that same year, Garnet Sloan left the Folk School to attend Seminary in Kentucky. When he left, there was no one to carry on the dance program throughout the year. Garnet had assumed this job voluntarily on the side from his weaving responsibilities, and there were no funds to hire a person specifically for dance.

For a time, it seemed that, except for the summer dance weeks, the dance program at the Folk School would be put into limbo. Marguerite and Otto again saved the day. "You can do it!" they both said. "You, Joe Wheeler, and Laura Sprung know enough about all of these dances that you can do it as volunteers." And so, with the Wood's help, Joe, Laura, and I carried on the Saturday night dances and even sometimes taught a beginners' class or two through the years until the dance program was stabilized once again at the Folk School.

In the spring of 1977, the word went around the community in early May that the Woods were back from Florida for the summer season. After a winter of dancing to recorded music, this news meant that the Saturday night dance would be packed with people, all eagerly awaiting the excitement of coming summertime activities.

Many people were already gathered at the Folk School dance hall when the Woods' Volkswagen drove up with Marguerite at the wheel. She got out and started into the door of the building, speaking with friends and leaving Otto to gather his fiddle and follow on his own.

We all watched as the passenger side door opened, and two wooden canes came out of the door. Otto pulled himself up and out of the car, gripped his fiddle case under one arm, and came, almost hobbling, into the hall. One hand firmly gripped each of the two plain wooden canes.

Everyone looked at Marguerite as if to say, "What's happening?"

She was never one to waste words on anyone, and this time was no exception. "Cancer," she said bluntly. "Might as well call it what it is. It took those doctors in Florida a long time to figure it all out."

As the summer unfolded, we all began to watch this little man, one whose life so bubbled over with activity and energy, as he tried to learn how to slow down. He was, this year, eighty years old.

Otto never missed a Saturday night dance. He would come and sit in a chair and play his fiddle, or he would lean on the end of the upright piano and play. Sometimes, he would call a singing square, but when he did, he simply called the dance without explaining any of the figures and dancers either had to know the dance or they were on their own when the music began.

As the summer went on, however, Otto seemed to get better. Friends and neighbors started to think him to be in some kind of remission.

One day in July, I decided it was time to go by for a visit. That's when I learned the truth.

I arrived at the Wood's house, and when Marguerite came to the door, I inquired about visiting with Otto. "He's out in the back," she announced. "Go right on through. He'll be glad to see someone else besides me."

I went through the house and out onto a kind of rock patio area that faced south. There, in the July heat of the sunny side of the house, I found Otto, stretched on a long, extended plastic lawn chair, wrapped in several blankets, shivering. The moment of real truth had arrived.

Marguerite had followed me out there, and as I looked at Otto, she spoke for him. "He's saving his pain medicine," she began. "He's been experimenting, and he's got it pretty well worked out.

"On Mondays, he leaves out one dose. Then on Tuesdays, he leaves out two doses, and on Wednesdays, he skips three. By Thursday and Friday," (it was a Friday afternoon when I was there), "he just fights it out through the day without any at all. It's all to get ready for the Saturday night dance, you see."

I didn't yet see. I just stood there in amazement and kept listening.

Marguerite went on. "On Saturday mornings, he takes a dose early. Then a little while later, he takes the next dose ... like I said, he's got the timing all figured out ... and he keeps taking more and trying to eat what he can for the rest of the day."

I was beginning to understand.

The next night, Saturday, when we all arrived at the dance, what we saw was Otto Wood walking in the door without even bringing his canes, playing music madly for two hours before he collapsed to start his regimen all over for another week. His playing for those dances was all the public ever saw of Otto's illness. After the dance, Marguerite took him home to preside over his planning for the next weekend.

The Wood's friends in Brasstown, those who lived there all of their lives, were stronger than their dear but seasonal friends on the Gulf Coast of Florida. The mountain people did not come and go when the seasons changed, and the Woods determined that Brasstown would be a better place to stay and be in one spot for Otto's medical care.

They did decide, though, that keeping up with their little house was too much. "We've never spent the winter there ...I'm not sure the house could take it!" Marguerite said. An arrangement was made for the Woods to move into a small apartment in Orchard House, a residential building on the Folk School campus. We were also aware that the Orchard House apartment was on level ground and only a few steps from the car while getting from the car into the Woods' own little house involved climbing both a small hill and several steps.

Their house was not actually put on the market. No, word simply went around that it was to be sold and that anyone who might be interested should stop by for an interview. Marguerite and Otto then began to decide who they would like to see living in their little house.

Among those who came by to talk about the house were Michael and Cathy Oliphant. Not long married at the time, they were young and with few resources. They had almost gone to the house as much to get to visit with Marguerite and Otto as with the real possibility of being able to make a home purchase.

When all of the visits and interviews were over, Michael and Cathy were the ones Marguerite called back. "You're going to buy the house!" she announced, then stated a price that was so absurdly low that it couldn't possibly be right.

"We won't take a penny less!" Otto broke in. "That's what it cost us to build thirty years ago and that's what we've got to get back out of it."

"Besides," it was Marguerite who finished the conversation, "We've lived in it and gotten most of the good out of it. It wouldn't be fair any other way." She was slyly grinning.

On that day, the Woods, who never had put much value in "buying things" and who had no children to whom they might leave anything, passed their values on to another whole generation.

October came and went, and, for the first time, Otto and Marguerite stayed on in North Carolina. They continued to play for the Saturday night dances past the Christmas season and into the beginning of the New Year.

It was one Sunday morning with snow on the ground, the morning after the last dance for which Otto would ever play, when he announced to Marguerite. "I want to go back to Florida and say goodbye to people there, Marge."

"When do you want to go?" she asked.

"I'm ready ... help me get to the car."

James Caldwell, a neighbor, volunteered to drive them on this trip. James would drive them down so that Marguerite could attend to Otto. Then he would take the bus back to North Carolina.

Two days after they got back to Florida, I received Marguerite's phone call: "Otto's dead!" Again, she did not waste words. "He got to visit around here a little, and then he was finished."

I never even had a chance to ask about funeral or memorial plans as Marguerite was already in the process of telling me what she had in mind.

"Not many of his friends are here," she said, "so I've decided not to waste him."

At this point, I had known this woman long enough not to even wonder what was in her mind. I simply waited and listened, knowing that she was about to tell me.

"I'm having him cremated, and we'll save the ashes for the summertime. Then, when I come back to North Carolina, we can have a dance and a big party, and everyone there will get a chance to say goodbye to Otto!"

Later in the spring of that year, when Marguerite arrived back in Brasstown, there, with all of her musical instruments, was a little brown box. On the lid, it simply said: "Last Remains: Otto Dale Wood."

Marguerite told me later that she had decided to keep

Otto in the sock drawer. "That's one drawer I open every single day," she reasoned. "That way I can speak to him, and he can speak to me." So, that is where Otto's remains lived.

One day some of the neighbor women organized themselves and came over to help Marguerite clean the apartment. When one of them discovered Otto's ashes in the sock drawer, she decided that Otto needed a better resting place. She removed his remains to a decorated cake tin and put him on the mantle. The problem was that she forgot to tell Marguerite.

For several days Marguerite said nothing. "I just thought that maybe I had misplaced him. I didn't remember throwing him out or anything."

Then the guilty ones heard of what happened, and they showed Marguerite where they had put Otto. Soon he was safely back in the sock drawer.

When summer came, it was time to plan the farewell party for Otto. Dance Week was the last week of June, and Recorder Week was the following first week of July. The plan was made to have a community gathering on the Saturday between these two weeks (some people could stay late after Dance Week, and others might come early for Recorder Week) to say goodbye to Otto. We would gather in the woods in a small area known as "Moulton Gardens," where Otto's ashes were to be placed under a rock on which there was a small plaque with his name.

Otto and Marguerite were Episcopalians, but she insisted,

"We are not Episcopalians with a capital 'P.' We're not silly about it. The priest will have to come, but we've already told him that you are the one who is going to say something about Otto ... not silly!" She was speaking for both of them still.

As the day approached, I began to wonder what I might significantly say about this dear little man, something not silly that would be a worthy memory of more than eighty years of life lived "doing things." Then, suddenly, an image came to me.

After Otto and Marguerite had taught me that I could call dances, I did that with regularity for quite a while, sometimes with them as musicians and sometimes with other people playing the music. The thing I suddenly remembered was this: with most musicians, the hardest thing to do while you were trying to teach the dance was to keep the musicians quiet so that the dancers could listen. Then, when you were all ready to dance, everyone had to stand and wait while those same musicians now had to take their own time tuning up.

It was, however, never that way with the Woods. They were always totally quiet while the caller was teaching, and then, they were totally ready to play when it was time to dance. I mentioned this to Marguerite: "I never remember having to wait for Otto to tune his fiddle when it was time to start the dance," I said. "I know that he was always in tune, but I never remember having to spend time waiting for him to tune up."

Marguerite laughed, "Oh, that's the way life is!" she started, "Some people tune, and some people play."

That moment, I knew, would become my forever memory of Otto Wood.

So, we met in the woods. We sang and danced our goodbye to a little man who used all of his life, in a metaphor that was larger than literal, playing his music.

Two years later, we met in the woods again. This time it was to say goodbye to dear Marguerite, whose own battle with cancer she had announced to us only months after Otto's departure. This time I could tell everyone the story of how Marguerite had told me what I could say when we were saying goodbye to Otto: "Some people tune, and some people play!" we could all repeat it together by now.

As with all friends who leave this earthly plane of life, I often go for extended periods of time without actively thinking about the Woods. Then I have one of those days, you know what I mean, when I spend the entire day "just tuning." Sometimes I can put several days of "just tuning" together. That's when I am called back to life by Marguerite's voice as I again hear her words, "Some people tune, and some people play," and those words give me a kick so good I can get right up and start playing my music.

If you have enjoyed this book

point your browser to:

www.parkhurstbrothers.com